HEAVEN'S
CONSCIOUSNESS

HEAVEN'S CONSCIOUSNESS

A NEAR-DEATH EXPERIENCE
with Relevant Poetry

RHONDA N. DOOLEY

History shows that the Bible has endured the natural digression of multiple languages. First, the Samaritan's symbols were recorded on tablets of stone. The Arabic and Hebrew language was written to Greek then to Latin and finally English.

I use the scripture to support what I experienced rather than the more common interpretation of the scriptures.

- The Old Testament books were all written between 1000–50 BC. Some of the accounts contained within these books are much older and existed as oral tradition before being written down.
- The Old Testament was translated into Greek around 200 BC. This Greek copy is called the Septuagint. This version became the primary copy of the Old Testament that the writers of the New Testament would have been familiar with.
- The Old Testament was comprised of the Torah (Pentateuch), Historical Books, Wisdom Books, and the Prophets.
- The Gospels, the Epistles, and the Book of Revelation were all written in the first century AD in Greek, hundreds of years after Christ.

Bible Scriptures are taken from the English Standard Version and King James Version.

ISBN: 978-0-9969391-0-2
ISBN: 978-0-9969391-1-9 (e-book)
Kindle ASIN: B00RZMESHC

Editor: Rachel Stone
Illustrator: Stephanie Grace Dooley Thompson

*To my beloved twins, Jonathan and Stephanie,
and to your companions and children.*

Acknowledgments

Rachel Stone, you are undoubtedly a life saver and a Godsend.

I am ever so grateful to my dear friends, Arlyn and Mitch, for being enormous blessings.

While in Heaven, I time traveled forward and saw my two darling, healthy twins. They both have very lovingly encouraged me by helping me write this book. Together, we have continued to experience the ever-increasing realization of our purposes in life.

Thank you all for your kind hearts and for helping me to be bold in my efforts to describe the most abstract dimensions known to humanity.

Table of Contents

Preface 1
Introduction 3

PART I: NEAR-DEATH EXPERIENCE 7
Chapter 1: Life before Death 9
Chapter 2: Out of Space and Time 13
Chapter 3: Light-years Away 17
Chapter 4: The Dark Side 21
Chapter 5: Blue Tunnel—White Light 27
Chapter 6: Watching over Me 33
Chapter 7: Heaven's Garden of Life 37
Chapter 8: My Spirit 41
Chapter 9: Before I Was Born 45
Chapter 10: One Life Review 49
Chapter 11: Exploring Paradise 55
Chapter 12: My Heavenly Neighbors 59
Chapter 13: Time Traveling: Levels of Heaven 65
Chapter 14: Heaven Is Orchestrated by Music 71
Chapter 15: Sometimes We Call Them Saints 77
Chapter 16: Beginning with Heaven 83
Chapter 17: The Center of Creation 91
Chapter 18: Looking Past Earth's Chaos 97
Chapter 19: Entering Earth's Galaxy from Paradise 103

PART II: LIFE AFTER DEATH 111
Chapter 20: Spiritual Awareness 113
Chapter 21: Mission on Earth from Paradise 121
Chapter 22: God's Breath of Life 125
Chapter 23: Science Has Come Full Circle 133
Chapter 24: Prayer: A Challenge for Science 139
Chapter 25: Trusting My New Paradigm 151
Chapter 26: Our Conclusion Is Heaven's Consciousness 157

GLOSSARY 167

RELEVANT POETRY

1. From Dust to Paradise 12
2. God's Vantage Point 16
3. Trust 20
4. Overcoming Fear 26
5. Near-death Experience 31
6. Welcome Home 36
7. Paradise Memory 40
8. Harmony with Heaven 44
9. Love Your Neighbor 48
10. Free Will Decides 54
11. Faith? 58
12. Deep Love 64
13. You Light Up My Life 70
14. A Jewel 76
15. Growing in Grace 82
16. Who Am I 90
17. River of Life 95
18. The Worldly Phase 102
19. Boldness Breathes Light 109
20. Divine Love 120
21. Opportunity Accepted 124
22. Timing 131
23. My Key 138
24. Intelligence 150
25. Precious Souls 156
26. The Mind of the Spirit 164

Preface

The presence of Heaven is right here on earth for you to personally appreciate from your own perspective. In her step-by-step account, Rhonda expresses with clarity the value of spirituality in today's world. She answers life's greatest mysteries, such as: Why are we here? Why is there so much suffering on earth? Viewing life through the lens of Rhonda's voyage through Heaven's consciousness, the cares of this life are understood with a new sense of hope, faith, and happiness.

Rhonda welcomes you to time travel along with her on a delightfully deep discovery that gives you a new understanding of life. You will receive a sweeter realization of your individual life's purpose. You may sense your own future while touring her lovely mansion located on the edge of the Garden of Life. Together, you will travel among intricate dimensions. From Heaven's throne flows God's breath of living water that creates musical varieties that orchestrates all of earth's creation. You will venture through the blue tunnel and may experience your White Light (Holy Spirit). You will travel through dimensions of timelessness into Paradise and visit where saints and hierarchies are dwelling with God. Rhonda provides practical insights to keep you grounded in a world of turbulent times.

Introduction

There are thousands of near-death reports every year in countries around the world that baffle even the best scientists and doctors. Up to this point, no scientific explanation has integrated spiritual truths into an understanding of this ongoing wonder. Thousands of documented near-death reports challenge mainstream Western thinking and belief systems. Love cannot be seen in a petri dish. The behavior of a living organism reacts to its environment, suggesting that its life has a form of consciousness.

Almost all who have a near-death experience (NDE) unexpectedly develop new spiritual abilities that offer insights concerning the purpose of life on earth. Science has made an important discovery that the conscious mind may not reside only in the physical brain. Many people who have had an NDE accurately describe events that occurred around their bodies when they were unconscious or even clinically dead. Some NDEs have revealed family secrets, such as the existence of a never-mentioned sibling. According to typical, modern, enlightened thought, these things are scientifically impossible.

What these skeptical modern thinkers lack is the understanding that Heaven was created first. Heaven is our spiritual life evolving into eternal Love. Self-awareness in spiritual realities includes being guided in protection. It is an indescribable sacred relationship that grows in the progression of divine Love.

On earth, our spiritual consciousness continues growing. Each individual is intelligently designed to transcend this material world and proceed to his or her own expression of true wisdom. To most, passing from life to death is receiving pure acceptance from angelic beings. The White Light is the essence of fulfillment known to many as the Holy Spirit. Our lives in the hereafter continue to spiritually evolve. Heaven's consciousness is peacefully guiding us to our original and intended domain, where in perfect harmony the Lord of creation reigns in Love.

During our experience on earth, we are becoming more alive in our spiritual reasoning. In preparation for our future, we are one in spirit, expanding our intelligence and expanding Heaven's universe. We are the result of our choices; we create human energy fields. When our spiritual consciousness is attentive to our eternal soul, we can open our minds to new realizations about our own lives. Here, our true self becomes aware of our individual value, and in our self-discovery, we find our higher consciousness is one with creation.

Our scientific forefathers came to the same conclusions as today's recent quantum theories. Socrates, Plato, Aristotle, Einstein, and Max Planck were all persuaded that our lives are divinely guided and influenced. Those who experience an NDE see this as common sense.

Our consciousness is continually ascending into higher dimensions in the White Light of everlasting life.

"We have the prophetic word more fully confirmed, to which you will do well to pay attention as to a lamp shining in a dark place, until the day dawns and the morning star rises in your hearts" (2 Peter 1:19).

I believe this is the beginning of the dawning of a new day. Accepting our eternal life in Heavenly places is an intelligent response to our Creator. As you travel with me through the portals of space away from time into your eternal domain, you will receive new understanding of your own spiritual consciousness.

My purpose in this life is now more in tune with my Creator's intentions. Each one of us is an exceptionally unique accent of spiritual truth in this opportunity we call life. My hope is that you fall in love with your everlasting genius; your Holy Spirit is your extension in Heaven.

I have written this book to stir spiritual insight, especially of those who are discovering life through the study of near-death experiences. I want to offer support to all who have survived near death. This is my big "thank you" to all who have had the courage to come forward and share their wisdom of life and death. I, too have emptied my heart and am left vulnerable for skeptics and critics to scorn.

Creation is becoming restless, and we can sense the wobble. The time is come for humanity to get back to the values of life. The more that we understand our spiritual soul, the more we enjoy our overall purpose, and the more peace and love we share. Because perfect Love casts out all fear, there is no fear in Heaven. Since God is the ultimate manifestation of perfect Love, Heaven's consciousness is far removed from the atrocities on earth.

There are no religions in Heaven, only relationships—each within one pure consciousness of Love.

PART I

Near-death Experience

1

Life before Death

"We came from a particular place in Heaven!" These were the first words that I spoke when I was revived. My new reality is my conscious entanglement with the universe. Heaven is what no human eye has seen, no ear has heard, and no human can conceive unless spiritually awake. As you read about my Heaven, please keep this passage in mind so you might better comprehend your Heaven. I have tried to describe my tour through Heaven in terms I thought best reflected the astonishing magnificence of the Creator. It is certainly way beyond humanity's limited love that we have on earth.

I remember enormous, graceful butterflies in Heaven. Heaven inspired my love for variety, especially in how life adapts and morphs until it fulfills its purpose.

For example: in the life of the eloquent monarch butterfly, I observed how morphing leads to elegance and liberation. Like our original eternal soul, the caterpillar is blind to the fact it will become a butterfly. On earth, the caterpillar instinctly adapts itself into another life form. Through generations, it shares its grand design.

By noticing this exquisite morphing process, I saw an example of the elaborate, mystical handiwork of creation; the work of a higher spiritual authority revealed by Love in the order of God's divine timing. I am neither a scientist nor a theologian. I am happy just to think rationally. In my sacred time, I have observed my own transformation. I see proof that my eternal spiritual nature is growing, forming a new life, just as a caterpillar does.

My mother told me my fellowship with Jesus began when my grandmother saw me for the first time when I was eleven months old. My grandmother was dying. Her last request was to see "little Nell." The hospital administrator would not allow a baby to be taken into my grandmother's room. Right before she took her last breath, her face was glowing with a big smile, and she sweetly said, "Oh, I can see Jesus. Little Nell is in the arms of Jesus. She is so beautiful!" I believe my grandmother is and always has been one of my many Heavenly witnesses who are always watching over me, among my angels, family, and friends.

I grew up in a middle-class neighborhood in Tulsa, Oklahoma, three blocks from Paul Harvey's childhood home. My parents loved Paul's messages. He earned notoriety for being the voice on twelve hundred national conservative radio stations. He coined the phrase, "And now you know the rest of the story."

I am writing to tell you the rest of the story. I share the most difficult subjects as I am reminded of a promise I made to God. When I was just a tot, on the way home from church, riding in the backseat of our family's station wagon, so small, all I could see were the stars. Looking up into the night sky, I said, "God, give me the tough jobs, the ones that others shy away from; you know, like cleaning the toilets."

After being a missionary for five years, I got married. My husband and I believed our marriage would bring us balance. We energized one another's competencies, filled in strengths that were lacking, and nurtured one another through prayer. We two became one as our spiritual sensitivity levels increased. We assumed each other's consciousness and hopefully stabilized one another.

Years later, I became pregnant with twins. In 1982, I fainted and woke up in an emergency center. At age thirty-two, I was considered a risky pregnancy. My husband and I had more zeal than discretion and more ideas about faith than wisdom.

Our trust in the tender growth of our twins brought us closer to the realization of how creation works in the spirit. Every day brought a new challenge. Whether growing up in an ultraconservative household or being pregnant with twins at age thirty-two, I learned to trust a Loving, higher authority. This is when and where my relationship with God began to bloom.

I had two little hearts taking shape in my womb. Exercise, a healthy diet, and most of all, hope, kept my heart in tune with God's Love growing within me. I knew everything would turn out okay. I was checked into St. Johns Hospital in Tulsa in November.

From Dust to Paradise
All of our dust will turn to ashes
Our hearts are filled with peace
In harmony there are no clashes
All contention will one day cease
Life receives a greater meaning
True Love finds no remorse
In the beauty of believing
Opens hearts to life's true course
Heaven welcomes our true essence
Love arises from the dead
Breath of life in our existence
Lifts each heart that looks ahead

2

Out of Space and Time

I followed my spiritual instinct, and peace ruled my heart. My first baby was born at 5:09 p.m. At about 5:35 p.m., after receiving a transfusion and more blood than my body could hold, along with the second dose of anesthesia, I said with all I could muster, "I am going to die!" I lay with my feet strapped in stirrups and a blood bag connected to my arm by a needle as my physical pain and five senses wilted. I drifted into unconsciousness. My weakness turned into bliss as I faded in and out of my body.

After the doctor held up the first baby, the medical team moved into high gear. There was a big rush to retrieve the second fetus. The second twin rested under my ribs and wasn't receiving oxygen.

Doctor Haswell said, "If the second baby doesn't have an oxygen supply, chances are it will be mentally challenged."

I asked, "You mean, retarded?"

Doctor Haswell, calm and sincere, looked into my eyes. He lowered his voice, looked over his glasses, and answered.

"Yes."

Medical personnel stood on both sides of my table as I began to fade. I heard, "Vital signs! Vital signs!" and I clinically died. They told my husband to leave the room. Leaning over my body were two physically strong technicians—a big man and a big woman. They took turns sharing what felt like rubber-booted clubs that were electrified paddles meant to resuscitate hearts. They both stood firm with big shoulders and bombarded me with crushing blows.

As I lifted out of my chest, I became interested in their faces. I recall looking closely at their two faces, observing the sweat dripping from their foreheads. In amusement, I began to examine the pulsing veins in the man's forehead as though looking through a magnifying glass. His pulse boomed through his veins on his forehead, as falling sweat rolled down his cheeks. Their urgent yelling continued.

I thought, "You all are being so unprofessional and I caused this!" I noticed the panic in their eyes. The woman and the man felt an extreme sense of responsibility.

"Give it to me! It's my turn!" the woman yelled. Their success ratios and professional careers were hanging in the balance.

I read their thoughts; I saw that my number would be on the wrong side of their stat sheets. I watched as they worked feverishly to get a pulse. I was thoroughly free from the clutter in my brain yet very concerned that I had upset everyone. I thought if I could tell them I was okay, they would be relieved.

I floated above the medical people who desperately moved about, taking turns over my body. The doctor stood quietly until most of the people left. I was up in the corner of the room, watching the technicians and the medical team as they left very solemnly.

Everything looked clear, very bright, highly magnified, and entertaining. I was amused at the white sheet over my body contrasting with the red puddle of blood under my table.

In a state of bliss, not fully aware of my condition, I became very concerned about the head nurse. I wanted to put her mind at ease. She had exhausted her efforts. I went to her because I had upset her. I went behind the nurses' station, where she shuffled papers. I tried to get her attention.

I said, "I'm happy and I feel fine. Everything is okay, and don't worry!"

She didn't respond. She continued to wonder, "What am I doing with my life? I told the doctors that that second dose of anesthesia was too much for the weight of that girl!" She pictured herself sitting at her kitchen table trying to deal with another lost life. I felt sorry I couldn't help her.

I went back into the delivery room. Dr. Haswell stood in the empty room, looking out the window. Medical staff came in to clean up or say something. Tired and distraught, his responses were brief. His whole paradigm was preserving life and preventing death.

He kept thinking, "I believe you are the God of the living." His prayer was, "We do not want to suffer the loss of a life. I preserved life as you gave me the power to do." It was as though he was waiting on something.

I decided to go to the waiting room where family and friends sat in silence. Unaware I was outside of my brain, I continued to talk with people. My mother-in-law sat, quiet for a change. She stared at the floor, biting her bottom lip.

My mother struggled to feel the correct emotion. She could not figure out what to say.

"Should I be sad for the loss of my daughter, or should I be concerned about where the baby boy will go?"

I tried to shake her to get her attention to let her know that "everything will be fine." I saw many faces frozen in sobriety. The air around them was gray. I saw dark, expressionless people sitting quietly.

The nurse who was in a state of remorse, the doctor who was questioning the law, and my family were all ignoring me. In this dimension, the halls smelled of grief. I saw dark clouds lurking over the heads in the waiting room. The group that had so eagerly awaited the twin's arrival sat quietly. I wanted to thank them for coming. Most of all, I wanted to let them know, "I am doing very well, don't worry."

I went from one to another but was unable to get any reaction. My mother reminded me of those times when I was a child and she had been too busy thinking to pay attention to me. My husband went to the hospital café to stay busy and to collect his thoughts. The associate physician left to go to one of his children's sports games. Since no one there would respond to me, I followed my spiritual intuition—I departed.

God's Vantage Point

As I gaze into the morning sky
The reflections of light blinds my eye
As the sun rises to make a skyline view
The colors are blended only as God can do
As the minutes go by, all the shades renew
From high into the universe to the morning dew
Inspiring my heart, Heaven is real, like I knew
My reward for believing, I feel Love coming through
Beauty touches our hearts as we accept what is true
Heaven is waiting and this is our personal preview

3

Light-years Away

True joy and peace went through me; I could move through walls without a problem. I went through the ceiling and noticed ceiling tiles hanging from the cement floor above. I saw the aluminum strips that connected the ceiling to the cement. I noticed the electric conduit that led to the lights.

Calm and curious, I roamed between the floors. I could hear the rumbling below. Since the fear of death is totally irrational, the idea of being dead was a faint impression that passed through my mind a few times. I was happy to be weightless and extremely vigorous. It dawned on me I was free to fly away. Drawn by a gentle flow, I didn't question it. I decided to look for the exit sign and follow the crowd. As I flew over the heads of visitors, I looked down the hospital hall for the light of day. Away I went.

I flew through the plate-glass doors as though I knew where I was going. I flew high above the buildings. I flew into an intersection and above and between two skyscrapers.

I thought, "Finally, I'm flying again, I knew I was meant to fly."

Still very amused at my liberty and clarity of mind, I lingered, at ease. I was entertained by my heightened aptitude and an ability to navigate by thought.

At dusk, I sat on the corner of a high-rise, looking down at an intersection when the lights were just coming on. I looked over the city at the skyline as if I had done this many times before. I was in my hospital gown.

"If someone saw me flying above them, I would be reported to the police!" I tried to keep my hospital gown closed with one hand as I directed my flight with the other.

"They'll send a helicopter after me," I thought. I felt a sense of urgency to get out of sight. I flew all the way around a skyscraper. "If I'm asked, what will I tell the police? How will I explain?" I decided to fly higher to get out of sight.

A wind current carried me toward a great, old landmark. I went inside. I was maybe in the attic; I closely examined broken ornate statues, looking beneath the deep cracks on the aged relics; I wondered why they seemed valuable. This church had stained-glass windows and decorative statues. Like a sightseer observing ageless remnants covered with cracked paint, I followed a presence into the sanctuary. I entered through the huge, white, cathedral ceiling. I floated high up to the top as I listened to the whispers of the people below. This was my first time visiting a Catholic church. (The Diocese was right next door.)

"Why am I here?" I asked, and then I felt weightless and wonderful in the midst of Heaven's messengers. I was hovering in the peak of the cathedral. I felt a big swoosh flying by. In this pure, sweet calm, I felt another luminous presence, then another. It was as though we were all on a mission.

I watched from the upper regions of the cathedral. I observed a loving spiritual presence coming in with people. I didn't know if they were angels or passed-on loved ones. The people below moved slowly, and the angelic light bodies up there with me streaked by faster than lightning.

A few visitors quietly walked in from the cold outdoors, lit candles, and left after a few minutes of prayerful reverence. Some walked in hopelessly and left hopelessly. There were people who stopped to kneel. I remember seeing for the first time people genuflect as they bowed before statues, and I wondered what they were doing. Their angels came in and waited in high places, listening and responding to their hearts' prayers—and then swiftly disappeared.

I felt a deep sense of assurance and a special, gentle, comforting awareness from the kindhearted. I knew some of the people below were unaware that their angels always returned with an answer.

As an elderly lady knelt down before an old statue to pray, I sensed her longings and desired to share with her the knowledge—and reassure her—that her angels were with her. I thought about her heart and looked for her connection with Heaven. In compassion and sadness, I didn't see her light. She prayed intensely out of despair; she was spiritually unaware. She seemed to be stuck in her human feelings.

My heart, in tune with compassion, aligned in communion with God for her to have a fresh awareness of her Heavenly helpers. I left there with an assurance that she would let go of her human feelings to find a new awareness of divine Love.

I hesitated by the old cathedral tower bell then passed over the city and the hillside. I swooped and glided in the high wind and went through clouds in the sunset. I paused, and happiness swept through my heart as I looked down over the valleys, high peaks, and waterways in a faint thought that I was free from my earthly body.

The oceans and glorious mountains looked soft with nature's gifts. The ground became too small to see. I was aware I was flying through clouds and flowing in the wind.

"I'm going higher than the birds," I thought.

I looked around for a jet or an airplane and saw none. It felt normal to be flying again as I glanced around the sun's vibrant reflections on fluffy clouds. *"For you have delivered my soul from death, yes, my feet from falling, that I may walk before God in the light of life"* (Psalms 56:13).

I thought, "I'm leaving earth with no concerns."

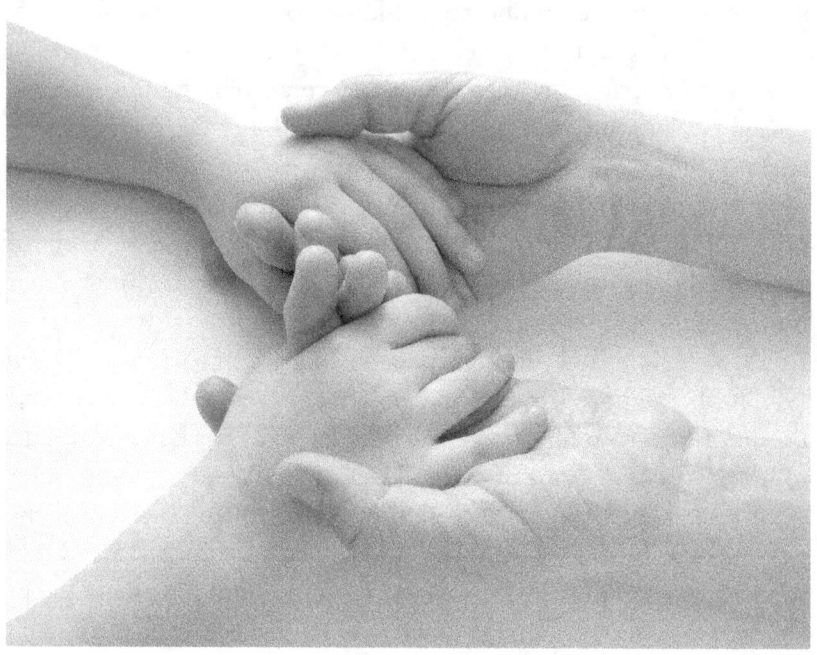

Trust

Trust is like a garment that covers us from the cold
Shelters from the night; tender as a child's hand we hold
Trust carries us into peace; priceless more than gold
Protects our heart from worry; cannot be bought or sold
Innocence learns trust is earned, perhaps lost when old
Trust understands true hope and honors love sincere
God's trust in us is our relationship and inherently near
Love replaces trust in us and shields us from all fear

4

The Dark Side

On my way to Heaven, I became aware that I was flying among living, intelligent lights. Death had no sting, no fear, and no remorse. Death brought immortality and liberation to my soul. I arrived where I saw spiritual consciousness in celestial countenances that shone brilliantly.

The way I saw myself changed with the consciousness in my surroundings. *"Giving thanks unto the Father, which has made us Light"* (Colossians 1:12). My environment was dark like the night sky, and I, too was in the form of a light orb, as was "everyone" around me. We were all in light formations going in the same direction. We all interacted telepathically, flowing together. I felt sensational currents like a loving hug—like many loving hugs.

Along the way, much larger orbs of consciousnesses had countenances that were very comforting. Their colorful messages radiated through me, intensifying my aura. My feelings were overwhelmed by multidimensional beings of a much-higher intelligence.

Just as I had done in my mortal body, I withdrew from crowded areas. I veered away from the traffic, as I would normally do. I felt alone, and my curiosity began to be aroused by an object in the distance. I noticed a small planet or a huge comet. From a distance, it appeared chaotic.

My attention was drawn by the first voice directed toward me since I had left my body. When I came closer, it took me by surprise. I looked toward the voice and felt an intrusive vibration, an intimidating tone derived from misery and hopelessness.

It sneered at me, "Get away from us; you don't belong here!"

I found my God-given light within; it stabilized me and allowed me to move forward and stay in unity. The voice that struck my soul with its hateful, attacking message caused familiar feelings to well up inside and made me recall the places where I had heard the distressing demand, "Get out of here; we don't like you!"

I was in a precarious situation. *"For God has not given us a spirit of fear but of power and love and self-control"* (2 Timothy 1:7). As usual, when I felt surrounded by negativity, my attention shifted to the center of my being where I found my aura in a gentle, peaceful light. This blinded my assailants. Then, I noticed angels were with me.

"There are two kinds of bodies, the glory of the Heavenly is one kind, and the glory of the earthly is of another" (1 Corinthians 15:40). Many specific instances flashed through my mind when I had been confronted with the same tone and personality.

"I have heard this tone way too many times," I thought.

The same words of rejection had followed me through my past life on earth. I realized the reason the angelic beings around me were unaffected by lower life forms—they were altogether in another dimension.

When the accuser projects malicious forces against the light of Heaven's consciousness, especially when I am in the flow of my Lord, it feels as though it is against me, personally. With the sound of that voice, my mind filled with many unfortunate events; for example, on my junior high school basketball team, certain girls had said, "You don't belong here! Get away from us!"

God's wonderful presence gets strong reactions, even from the dark side. Instinctively, my consciousness was lowered into an urge to retaliate. My choice came from my consciousness to make an effort to search for rational thought. My only other alternative was to turn toward the light surrounding me.

Everyone encounters degrading personalities; the Bible calls them "principalities and high powers of wickedness in high places" (Ephesians 6:12). I found my heart and soul in a very high place, confronted by a dark, raspy, voice that had been directed at me to disrupt my spirituality.

There are many kinds of personalities from various cultures in this multidimensional spiritual realm. I am happy to know my God's nature is Loving, brilliant, and wise, and most of all— protective. My spiritual awareness aligned with my Creator's spiritual connection within, and I found my pilot light, my belief in a faithful God. My courage came from a much-higher Source, one who is interconnected with me and who knew me in the depths of my soul.

Fulfilled with understanding and assurance, I then looked on as an observer. I had received precisely what I had needed—strength in the light.

Moving along, I saw a frustrated imp sitting on a drab, dark, very dry, dirty, gray rock. Its words had pierced my soul. Rather than retaliate, I looked past the problem. At first, it appeared to have something in its lap, a garment it was endeavoring to stitch. I thought maybe it was trying to sew its wings. It was with other imps that were chattering like a group of discontented women.

I reasoned within, "It thinks that by sewing its wings, it will be able to fly. It's trapped here!"

I heard other imps yelling at the one that caught my attention. Their tone was similarly degrading to one another. It became clear to me that they were competing and striving to fly while in a state of delusion. They were driven by an insatiable hunger to acquire freedom as their fulfillment. They think that to fly is the ultimate goal. Their intentions were to gain power without knowledge, authority without respect, and liberty without honor.

On my way to Heaven, I acknowledged the power struggle in earth's galaxy. Finding my weaknesses, I felt fairly inadequate to interact with suffering and hostility. I reached to find a new depth of my intuition. I turned inward to my soul, where I found a reservoir of courage.

As the saying goes, "It came to pass."

While I passed their stress and strife, I understood that conflict comes from separation. Detachment causes blindness, which leads to an anxious mind-set. Light made the contenders more miserable as we burned away the dark clouds of delusion and exposed their desperation. They were reminded of their miserable habitats; they hated the light of truth. Many more congregated, like an army of imps, all with large, black eyes.

Their looks projected a defenseless and seemingly harmless, curious glare, very alluring. I noticed that they were searching my heart, trying to make a connection, trying to steal my light. At the moment that I acknowledged their motive, I felt their fear. They were questioning my faith within. As their eyes searched me, I could see that their intentions were to challenge my peace. I thought of my courage as guttural fortitude. I found my soul interacting with my Holy Spirit. This brought me into a sense of fearlessness and boldness; I knew that I was protected from their attempts to steal my light and from their fear. A soldier once said that there were no atheists in foxholes. I held my emotional balance like a tightrope walker.

I recall thinking, "I love the light within the breath of me. I found my faith within."

I had peace that passed all understanding. I overcame fear by accepting my frailties, and most importantly, trusting that my life had a greater purpose. I found boldness in my belief. My Creator's purpose is in my realization of being loved when in harm's way or confronted by opposition. As I centered within my soul, my Holy Spirit came to meet resistance like a bug zapper. With a sense of going in the right direction, I found closure.

***

Behind me was a very large, masculine angel who resonated peace through his golden garment. His robe appeared to be very thick, heavy, decorative lace. Our interaction was in precision timing and instantaneous as we glided together. I was receiving clean, pure consciousness.

He conveyed, "Go forward." He was very strong and gave me confidence. His eloquent conveyance centered me in clarity, a telepathic flow of great strength. *"Behold, I send an angel before you to guard you on the way and to bring you to the place that I have prepared"* (Exodus 23:20).

In looking back, I believe I was being escorted by Archangel Michael's finest troops. It was as though I had traveled through here many times before.

I noticed other people around me as we approached the entrance or passageway. My self-perception adapted with my environment. I was standing with a few onlookers. We were as relaxed as if we were in an elevator. In hindsight and at a distance, the blue tunnel looked to me like a root of the Tree of Life (Genesis 2:9).

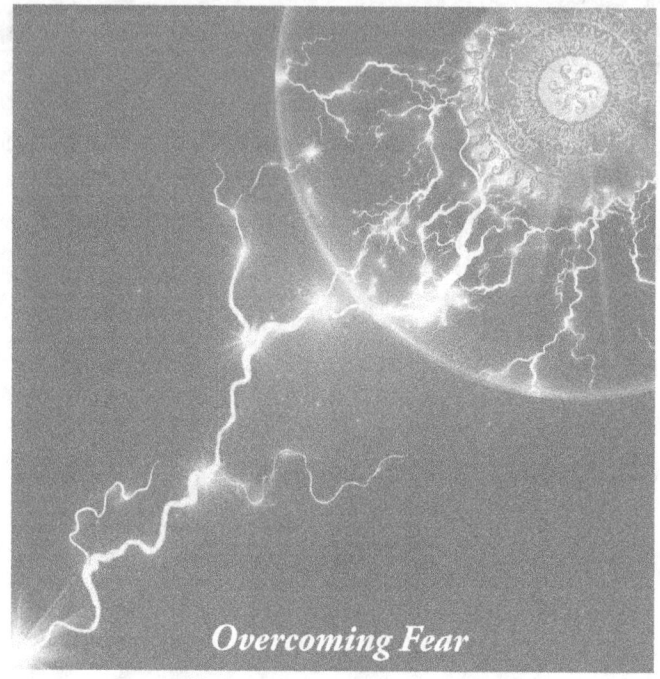

Overcoming Fear

I flew through barriers strong
I felt challenges I knew were wrong
Many criticisms came along
This heart of mine began a song
I listen to interpret well
What separates me from hell
And breathes a rhythm into me until
More excellence yet to find
Who I am in strength of mind
Retaliations left far behind
Inside this bosom where I live
Courage wells up for me to give
Fear is lost where Love is found
Our souls' Love is Heaven bound
All else is left upon earth's ground

5

Blue Tunnel White Light

Heaven's consciousness drew me higher. We approached an area that was a pure, clean, blue vortex in motion; it had facets like a diamond, yet its motion continued in symmetry.

I looked around, and there were people coming from other directions. Heaven's passageway, or blue tunnel, was a symmetrical entryway on the root system of the Tree of Life. I stood in wonderment on the verge of one dimension about to be introduced to the future.

Now, I am in full assurance of being in the presence of a peaceful, Loving environment. I felt myself being guided forward. I hesitated, acknowledging the significance of another heightened level of intelligence before I went in. A few of us stood outside, observing one another's reactions. I noticed we looked and felt naturally lighthearted, enthusiastically sharing a mind-set of wonder and discovery. I stood there, still holding my hospital gown together. I noticed a young child and a boy standing with me. We pondered going through into another realm. While we hesitated, at least two other people passed by us.

When we entered through the portal, we rode a current as if surfing a wave. The walls in the root of the Tree of Life looked like shiny, wet, sky-blue foam. The passageway was about three to four feet wide, large enough for only one other individual to pass at a time. There were people in front and behind me. We were all dressed, and we were all headed in the same direction. We flew, fully aware of one another, and in the unity of our collective consciousness.

A young man wearing jeans and tennis shoes passed me. He stammered, and his whole body shuddered as he went by. I felt for him as a mother who would want to protect a son. I reached out to grab his shoe, but a lady right behind me stopped me.

"Let him go on."

It never dawned on me that he might have been dying. It occurred to me the lady behind me might be his nurse, so I didn't disturb his struggle.

A huge wind swooshed through us.

I thought, "Oh, the rush of wind is to help us get to our destination!"

The lady in white behind me said that the wind was the power of prayer from earth. *I did not think anyone would be requesting our return.*

I received cooperation in its purest form. Without worries, we flowed together as in one stream of consciousness. The only individual emotions I felt were caring ones, like the concern I had felt for the boy. I was acutely aware that with no verbal exchanges; we were communicating thoughts through intelligent, emotional reflections.

I saw a gleam coming from a White Light. Love was penetrating, comforting light from an archway ahead. In my coherent thought process, I felt much more in tune with pure consciousness. This light was connected to my faith; it appeared to be about the size of a mustard seed (Mark 4:31-32). The brilliant White Light filled me with Love and kept my full attention as it seemed to be drawing me upward. I felt the presence of a Love that I had longed for.

My eyes adjusted to the bright light and I blindly fell into Love. "For judgment (pure consciousness) I come into the world, that they, which see not, might see; and they, which see, might be made blind" (Matthew 9:39). Brilliant Love waves of White Light blinded me and melded me into a unifying Love. I was being transformed from my individual spirit into perfect harmony, becoming one in Spirit. *"I am the way the truth and the life: no one comes to the Father except through me"* (John 14:6).

I merged into one solitary atom with all of Heaven. My realm of spiritual understanding became more thorough than I had ever known.

My capacity to grow in relationships expanded with freedom and clarity. My spiritual emotions were refreshed with sounds that awakened me to Heaven's perfect rhythm, all blending together as one. I had capacities I was unaware that I possessed and fresh feelings. My emotions awakened to majestic music moving in arrays of lovely colors. Joy rang through the rhythm of my soul, increasing the melodic sensations through all of our consciousnesses.

Tranquility and a multidirectional vision extended my sensory perceptions without limitation. My heart was renewed in a delightful flow of colorful tones. Everyone shared generous emotions, each with our unique, lively expression. Together, we were emotionally dancing within our glow and grace. In concert, we all increased the harmonics in one another.

I was reminded of precious words written about light on the *tablets of my heart:* "But whoever does what is true comes into the light, so that it may be clearly seen that his works have been carried out in God" (John 3:21).

I did not see an individual or one celestial being that stood out from the rest. A group of pleasant greeters gathered around the entryway. All of my earthly expectations diminished into overwhelming sensations of the pleasures of many perfect and Godly relationships.

The thought of a preconceived image of God, Jesus, or a saint did not enter my mind. Our Heavenly families greeted us, and we all wore lighted robes. To me, we were all an expression of our Lord. Our white robes reflected colors, conveying the messages of each unique soul. We all went through a sanctifying white fire, the Holy Spirit's light filter that thoroughly renewed our minds. I must have been born again —we all shared in one orchestration, each adding to one another our soul's expression of Immanuel or God with us.

As I entered, I became perfectly sensitized to new colors, fragrances, and the realization that my spirit added to the living structures—Heaven's marvelous righteousness in perfect and divine Love. I had no hidden thoughts. I flowed through Heaven's portal and became one with Love's grand design. My life was not all mine anymore.

I felt the fulfillment of being a valuable tone swinging within the vibrato in Heaven's symphony. More and more, Love encompassed me. In the midst of our spiritual clarity, we all knew we were extensions of one another. My finite soul awakened to unknown gifts within me wonderfully orchestrating new life. We all were stimulating one another with our thoughts through luminous colors. Eyes have not seen nor have ears heard of the glorious friendships that await us. Every instance was new, precious, and inspirational.

Pleasing music moved with our thoughts telepathically. Inside the city, I saw massive buildings with engraved detail around the tops and built by a powerful, dignified Lord. Huge gold blocks reflected lights that continually changed color with the music. The entire atmosphere was bursting with life, which seemed to produce new colors all around. The streets were transparent, golden-white streams, glimmering reflections of intelligence. Over the clear, fresh stream grew multicolored trees bearing fruit. Creation's Living water is God's Spirit of life. Heaven's glorious music was permeating creative intelligence.

Near-death Experience

God's Love reached out as the light called to me
Took my attention to the stars as far as I could see
Then, I looked around me at a world of debris
Then, I looked up into the White Light of pure ecstasy
As if to ask the master, "What do you ask of me?"
My focus was taken into the white fire of a new galaxy
I felt chilled as darkness is consumed by light
Foreboding as the sun swirls in the night
Gravity and matter held me in place
Awakened by God's Love, my connection of grace
God's presence drew me into a Love Heavenly
Creation reveals God's spirit divine
Now in the White Light, Heaven is mine
Enveloped in pure Love, unaware of space-time
Heaven's consciousness is my true paradigm

6

Watching over Me

I saw a very happy group of dear friends wearing glowing clothes coming toward me, or I was moving toward them. All welcoming thoughts intertwined as I remembered their faces. Each one was kindred, sensible, and extremely resourceful. We were all friends and family. We all came from the same neighborhood—our ancestral tree. We were all familiar and full of enthusiasm and precious in our own way. My dear friends knew me in ways I didn't even know myself. Our many lives that took place on earth were preparation for our everlasting futures. My gentle grandmother, my caring uncles, relatives, and special friends all embraced without words but with a deep, bonded relationship.

I thought, "My friends are my 'angels.' I have known their presence as I know my own soul."

The overall message was approval in its fullest sense. We shared in vivid clarity and exchanged new feelings. We were one family, comfortably home. I knew that together, we were the rock of stability for one another.

Also, many times in my life I had trusted a sixth sense of when to utter a firm no without having to rationalize or justify my decision. I had incidences and images come to mind when I had made intuitively based decisions. In Heaven, it was obvious to me that my insightful relatives—Heaven's consciousness—were my spiritual hierarchy. I remembered on earth when I knew that I had help from above as events fell into place, only shown to me in the secret chambers of my heart.

On earth, when I had made loving, intuitive decisions, everything always worked out and everyone was pleased. I had felt a sense of certainty that I relied on; an inner knowing of doing good that I had followed. Throughout the years, people said I was gifted. *"When a man's ways please the Lord, he makes even his enemies to be at peace with him"* (Proverbs 1:7).

On earth, I found solace listening to Heaven's council aligning with God's wisdom. This is where I could easily contemplate and find comfort in identifying my own self and accept that my soul held my own living "truth." I found special, sacred places where I communed with God. I loved climbing and sitting high up in the treetops to rest and contemplate life. This was where I learned to listen to and trust my heart. On the roof of my childhood home, my little feet wore a path to my hiding place next to the fireplace chimney.

As a young girl, life's hard knocks taught me to look past my impulsive, emotional reactions and center myself with my intuitive, inner knowing; I found fresh, new strength within my soul.

My first-grade teacher, Mrs. Rushmore, published one of my poems in her book of children's poetry. I recalled having artistic ability that amazed my art teacher and myself. When I was a fifth grader, I made amazing art. Using acrylics, I drew what I thought was a pretty bird of Paradise. My art teacher said that I painted an excellent Phoenix. Two of my paintings hung in the Museum of Fine Art in Tulsa, representing Jefferson Elementary School.

I was taught in Sunday school that some of my words came from the Spirit. Other times, answers to the questions that people were looking for just came to me. I was the family's "go to" girl to find things that were lost. Creative imagery came time and again from my Spiritual family. I knew deep in my heart that I had help from above.

I amazed even myself when writing poetry, painting a picture, and solving problems. Whether practical or purely inspirational, I trusted an intuition in my heart. Trusting in my Spiritual help, I accepted life's challenges. I exhibited boldness that amazed people; they called me lucky. But I knew luck had nothing to do with it. I thanked nurturing friends who taught me discretion in their gentle ways—when to keep still and when the time was right to boldly respond.

Overall, it wasn't about who did what or when but rather about my situating my life so that I could listen well to my Loving premonitions. In this process of self-discovery, I was also exploring Heaven's consciousness.

Whether faith, intuition, artistic gifts, or spiritual aptitude—my creative abilities came from being in tune with my higher consciousness. We are one in Spirit together through our lives.

At times on earth, it was easy to feel lonely. I am sure that every friend in Heaven was reaching out to me all the way through my lifetime.

Welcome Home

In divine order Love is our original purpose
God's wonderful ways make us courageous
Our Love light empowers our living universe
Opens our hearts and inclines our minds
We see our Love light intertwined
In divine rhythm where arch angels reign
In due course, we arrive from whence we came
We're going home to our original domain
We shall arrive in Heaven again

7

Heaven's Garden of Life

In Heaven, our consciousness is much greater than it is on earth. In the distance, I saw an enormous choir. Music surged through everyone's essence, stirring reactions throughout and increasing a calm yet ecstatic thrill. Our personas were reflecting tones, each blending our own colorful expression. Our beings were radiating our thoughts like the fragrances of enormous flowers beaming their gentle aromas.

I saw large, flying, gigantic butterflies, and elegant, winged animals that were delightful and friendly. Music, in a liquid composition, streamed through everyone and everything.

Coming from the throne, the fountain created golden streets. Aligned with the waterway was channeling the volume of the music throughout Heaven. God's consciousness moved our individual thought processes with flavor and wonder. Our reactions synchronized with the music.

My attention shifted to a branch. A flourishing tree brimming with charm hung over the stream. I noticed a variety of fruits and various kinds of blossoms on the same branch. I knew the food was delicious, although I was so awed by the massiveness of the tree that

I didn't taste the fruit.

I saw bright, glistening gemstones that moved with personality. Perhaps they were living, growing, evolving souls like shells and other life forms in the living water. I gazed at the living stones that were projecting colors, and I noticed that they were growing because of my attention.

I thought, "All of these are like Heaven's seeds, conscious of their lives, although without a free will. My intelligence is resonating with them."

It was a new realization: as I gave my attention to the lesser life forms, a connection was established. I drifted down the thoroughfare, amused at the tranquil progression of *everything*, interconnected and alive. I watched children slide around in open blooms of soft, bright flowers. I was amused at the flowers that were large enough to be a playground. Childish giggles rang out as the little children shared their love with life-sized pets.

I casually said, "They are in their play park."

I set down by a building with a cute puppy that seemed to be following me. I stopped to think, and I looked at the grass, remembering the ground on earth and thinking in the same clarity.

I remembered that on earth I had longed to be in such a harmonious orchestration. I rested as I pondered.

"I have always been in the process of moving forward for a higher cause. I have never been alone. Our lives are intertwined, the very essence of one another's."

Though I will always be expanding with creation, in each phase I find my development is like a baby's; during each stage of growth, I am perfectly whole.

My friends and I created new harmonic frequencies. Heaven's music was continually bringing our excellence to the surface. It seemed as though this was the height of my spiritual journey, although I was in the very beginning of my Heavenly tour. I continued to ponder, remembering my past life here.

"Earlier, I played with life-sized pets. I loved to slide around on soft petals into the heart of a flower. I remember riding on big butterflies, flying through the mist of waterfalls."

With my longtime, precious friends—each one a unique neighbor—we gave our own special kind of Love to our Garden of Life. I found my heart flowing in a deep genuine Love from the heart of Creation. We adorned everything in gracious blends of living colors and ever-changing tones, each one a conscious reflection of our environment's joy.

To my surprise, all the plants, animals, and all the other living things supported and nurtured me in response. Even the flowers that decorated the lighted waterways smiled as I passed by. We all added our own variety, sharing our own unique bliss. In Heaven's sensational music, our colorful auras were increasing and intensifying.

I was developing an even deeper sense of gratitude. We all added graciousness and goodness by contributing to one another. I had an overwhelming sense of excellence, being valuable in the process of an evolving Love.

In Heaven, the plants and animals were alive and moving together. The essence of our Love toward one another moved in a concentrated rhythm in adoration for life. As friends' and relatives' consciousnesses merged, we knew the origin of our connection.

Thoughts increased the sound of the music and added to the enthusiasm in Heaven's consciousness always increasing impulses and spiritual emotions. We were at peace and as one, intertwined in the pulse and rhythm of Heaven.

Some of us had returned from earth with an extended awareness of the central character of the universe. In a deeper sensitivity, we arose to every occasion with a gentler, inner knowing and appreciation for life. We expanded during our earthly experience, developing new strength. Resiliency from souls sprang forth, refreshing fountains; we were increasing the wealth of Heaven's flourishing fruitfulness. Each one a radiant prism growing on the Tree of Life. In the network of divine intelligence, we shared God's multidimensional Love.

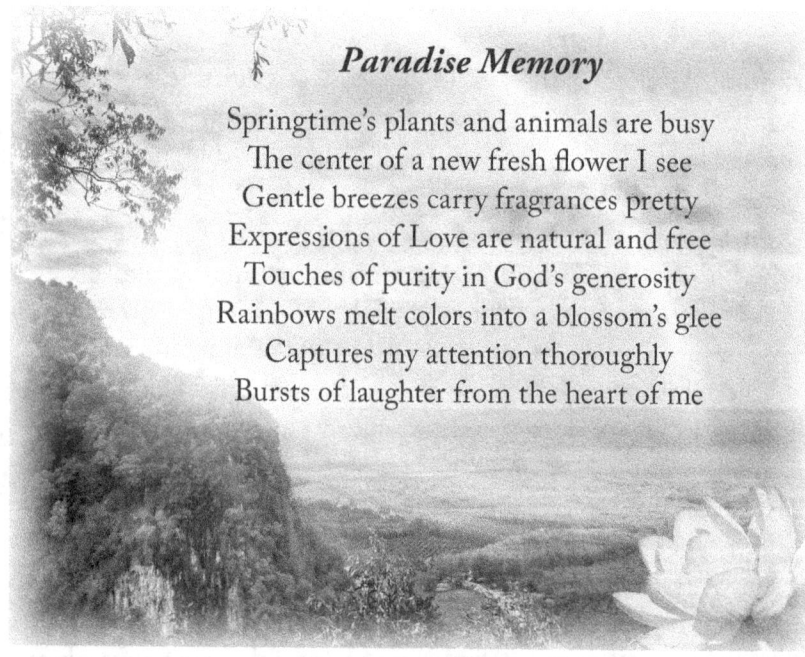

Paradise Memory

Springtime's plants and animals are busy
The center of a new fresh flower I see
Gentle breezes carry fragrances pretty
Expressions of Love are natural and free
Touches of purity in God's generosity
Rainbows melt colors into a blossom's glee
Captures my attention thoroughly
Bursts of laughter from the heart of me

8

My Spirit

I met my higher self in the form of God's Holy Spirit; my gift was shown before me in the form of a silver cloud. God's presence fills my conscience. My manifestation of God's promise is to be one with all Heaven's beloved. My thinking felt perfectly thorough; I found the seat of my soul, my eternal self, in my peaceful resting place.

My true essence, my omnipotence, is an extension of the omniscience of my Lord. When the cloud moved, I moved, and when it stayed, I stayed. My spirit moved as one with my visible cloud of God's presence (Exodus 40:34).

In the ambiance of my gentle influence, my higher intelligence, I had vivid clarity; I became completely absorbed in my Heavenly silver cloud, always together as one. In some esoteric way, I AM an extension of the all-knowing and unlimited, divine and pure cognitive expression in Heaven's Omnipresence. Although I was perfectly whole in as far as I already had ascended, I am growing into my fullness, continuing forward, evolving in pure consciousness.

My questions are answered in lighted, colored currents, bright streaks connecting our beings. I could see my own thoughts and those of others in the form of colored lights creating waves, increasing the music as they moved between us. Happily interacting in smooth discourse, I watched our thoughts cause motion throughout our entire bodies, not just in our heads. Our thoughts were arranged in vivid colors like bright-colored lightning. Beams glanced with our thoughts through our whole beings. Each color was a feeling, a dialogue with imagery waving through my intuition. Intimately aware of every aspect of my life, I was known well in the fullness of my soul.

In my gift of God, I felt that my uniqueness, my individual personality, came across as very entertaining. While I lived on earth, my higher-spiritual self lived in the extended cosmos. I was sure that the extension of my soul knew God in a more thorough way. As I became more receptive, my soul grew to understand about life. I was sure we began as one at the conception of our lives. I knew that we were created to move in the orchestration of God's heartfelt circulation. Our thought processes were instantaneous, too intimate and sensitive for introductions. I was thoroughly fulfilled. *"All these are empowered by one in the same spirit, who apportions to each one individually as he wills"* (1 Corinthians 12:11).

It felt as though my probing mind was empowering my higher-spiritual consciousness, propelling my sense of direction and that of the others as well. I was the instigator, navigating our path in a passion to understand the purpose for life on earth. High above, the music came from rivers of living water carrying creative consciousness in its currents. My reward for maintaining my mental focus came in the discovery of my ability to expand my consciousness. My conversations with others were spontaneous, calmly void of a rational ability to arrange or select methods of communication.

I passed an entryway of a huge building with very large round columns. I pondered the massive size of the building and the group of enlightened celestial beings that stood in front of it. I continued moving away from them into a quiet area free from distracting interaction. I went to a place where I was on my own. I was no longer aware of my helpful guide.

I was shown my life from my first glimpse of my consciousness. This life review took me back in time to before I had an earthly identity. I went into a void where I found myself in clean, dark air. My consciousness included my whole environment in a new way. There shone before me glistening, living gemstones.

My lifetime on earth had enlarged my garden. It was flourishing, covered with my character as far as I could see. I hovered over rows of living, multifaceted jewels that only I had made. When I picked them up one at a time, my life review began, beginning before I ever was born. I went into the past to see how to improve my future.

Harmony with Heaven

I heard a beautiful melody echo through a chime
Music that soothes my soul is gentle on my mind
I felt a healing oil flow through every crevasse it could find
A peace hushed my senses as I drifted to unwind
Brought a whole new love for music and in a perfect time
I rest in wonder of sweet music and in perfect rhyme
I enjoy their sweet rhythm in amplified, pure sound
Heaven's angels touch my heart to keep me Heaven bound
Written on my heart are praises, I hear the lyrics of a song
In harmony with Heaven's choir, angels sing along

9

Before I Was Born

I experienced my life before my choice to be born. I began my review in a deep discussion, reasoning together with my Lord.

I am thoroughly incapable of conveying the gentle justice flowing in the wonderful heart of our Lord. God's Loving heart is inexplicable, so intimate, so sensitive that words or human energy fields— in the form of human sound waves—could interrupt the pure divine order of our Creator. Yet, in the pure consciousness of my Holy Spirit, I am aligned with this virtue in creation.

"No man has ascended into Heaven unless he has descended from Heaven" (John 3:13). As I dwelt within the tenderness of my Lord's heart, I conceived an opportunity for a life on earth. God shared with me a "free choice" to develop by imparting to me my free will to spiritually evolve within creation's intelligent design.

The saints that were around me had evolved in spirit and shone brightly. They flowed within God's optimum happiness and wisdom. They communed in smooth discourse with the Most High. I, too, knew that God's Love was continually perfecting my spiritual consciousness. I became receptive and willing to enter into the secret chambers of my Creator's council, where all relationship decisions are Love covenants.

I realized my life's purpose was to create a fresh, new individuality, unique in divine Love unlike any other in my celestial family, where there is no fear, conflict, or regret. It was my turn to expand Heaven's consciousness.

God's Holy Spirit prepared me to enter into higher dimensions where Love's clarity becomes creative. I desired to bloom and evolve with God's beloved saints and progress with my Heavenly family. Now, in the presence of omniscient Love, the only kind of decision is a covenant promise. I chose to go to earth and fulfill my life's purpose in grace and the light of Heaven.

"Before I formed you in the womb I knew you, and before you were born I consecrated you; I appointed you a prophet (a spiritual voice) to (your families) the nations" (Jeremiah 1:5). As I pondered my thoughts, I found my heart saying, "Daddy, when I grow up, I'm going to be big like you."

My life on earth would be a glimpse of eternity, temporary from Heaven's vantage point. I had passed through hidden in darkness, and was ready to emerge with the winds of the season in the Holy Spirit. A phase of earth life, an orientation in a cycle of time, would allow me to receive grace, to eventually be more creative, growing in perfect Love.

I became as a little child under the shadow of the Almighty. I reasoned with God in Spirit, my source of life. All my decisions were laid out before me. In Heaven, where the chaos and the limitations of earth are incomprehensible, my value is in the depths of true Love.

This is all there is that is comprehensible; my soul growing in wisdom in the perfection of the Creator's Love while building eternal relationships.

I did not choose a physical womb or my nationality—Scotch, Irish, or Norwegian—nor did I select my O negative blood type. I did ask for a particular placement where, through my willpower, I would become readily available for my soul to grow.

From Heaven's vantage point, all learning opportunities begin as minuscule mistakes, like finding your balance when you fall or correcting a wrong turn.

My Heavenly consciousness will help me in my formation of God's character. The short life cycle on earth would evolve my soul to eventually create with the saints in the midst with the Most High. I decided to move forward.

In earth's life cycle, I decided to be given a life that would challenge me: I was given a choice of accepting a challenging life. I saw I would evolve a more creative willpower if I chose the rough road. My difficulties on earth would be finite in comparison to the grace that I would develop in my spiritual journey. With a free choice, I would reach for the more excellent way. I would learn how to develop good habits and choose my lighted path by listening well to my conscience.

My characteristics were preset—much like a seed's are before it is planted. God's Spirit made the unique character of a seed. God gave the seed its life through creation (Isaiah 61:11). I responded to the delightful nurturing of the Spirit, just as the seed responded to the sun and water.

I understood that in earth's timeline, I would not be able to recall my Heavenly choices. I was shown I would be unable to remember my original existence because to be nurtured by the White Light of pure Love, I needed to be fully reliant in a trust relationship with the *author and finisher of my faith*.

So, I opened my heart to learn how to trust for the intervention of Heaven while in earth's timeline. I was far removed from humanity's limitations, yet very sensitive to the actual reality of my spiritual life process.

In my little, untarnished mind, I had spiritual clarity. My decision was supported by Heaven's consciousness where every living thing is progressing and continually evolving. I reasoned within the council of God's pure heart. I conceived my gift of the Holy Spirit when I willingly accepted God's everlasting Love covenant. Bonded in oneness, I will be growing in our faithful relationship. My Lord is my Holy Spirit evolving in the righteousness of God's will. My gift expands my understanding to willingly receive pure consciousness trusting Love's justice to devise my way.

Love Your Neighbor as Yourself

As we understand, our spirit becomes aware
Our vicinity in eternity, perfection in the air
Heaven's consciousness is our neighborly affair
Our soul on earth is in Heaven's care
Our neighborhood is our spiritual sphere
Our personal angels show us where
Through out the ages, in freedom we share
While we live here we also live there
Our life on earth is our eternal prayer
This overwhelming reality is extraordinaire
Our exact location is with our Heavenly neighbor
We are one in God's Love evolving together
Loving your neighbor is loving yourself
In our hereafter

10

One Life Review

My Book of Life is all that I was and all that I am to be, now open before me. I looked into the distance and saw an enormous garden. Rather than fresh produce in a spring garden, my garden grew all kinds of jewels, crystals, and gemstones. Some were brighter than others, but all were stunning. On the edge of one corner, I hovered over a lifetime of past choices. The ground was soft and light brown, like powdery earth. I could choose from many rows of glistening jewels of distinct colors. I knelt to observe the details of my life and relive one event at a time by choosing what to examine. Each row was decked with pretty ornaments and labeled with years, months, days, and seconds.

I looked into the reflection of one jewel and entered into the space and time before I was born. There were incidents in each cut of the jewel. Some shimmered brightly; others were dim and dull looking. It wasn't about being good or bad but rather seeing the more excellent way to fulfill life's purpose.

In cognitive light, I saw how my actions affected others. I was free to pick up any jewel and look into it like a window into the past. In each gem, I could see into my soul that a lesson was learned. I saw a life of free options that formed my Heavenly signature. I visited optimal moments of my spiritual formation.

One minor detail that I thought no one would remember brought substantial nourishment to my garden's growth. In my amazement, I pondered how my personal, silent wishes became embedded in the Garden of Life, designing my future in Heaven's consciousness.

In my effort to understand my feelings, I learned that by controlling my thoughts, I could be more aware in the present tense. Though insignificant on earth, my thoughts were colossal in Heaven. My simple, good intentions enlightened others around me with the vitality of life (Isaiah 58:11).

In one incident, I saw an old man working hard under the hood of an old truck in the heat. He kept wiping his head with a hanky. I felt sorry for him, thinking that he must have been thirsty. I scooted a dining room chair to the sink, as I was too short to reach a clean glass. I took a fruit jar from the counter and filled it with water. Every drop was significant. I held the jar with both hands as I carefully walked down the back steps. Very slowly, I took it out to him.

He bumped his head on the hood when he heard me say, "Sir, are you thirsty?" I could hear how my voice sounded to him. I must have answered his prayers. He drank it down in one gulp. I think I enjoyed that water as much as he did.

He smiled at me with a very appreciative smile and said, "Thank you, sweetheart."

In another incident, I gave my tricycle up to an older boy after he intimidated me. I had to learn not to listen to the tone of intimidation.

I revisited the experiences that led me to better understand how my subtle reactions helped shape others' futures as well as my own: In a long line, I let a school bully cut in front of me without telling. He was shocked that I didn't retaliate. I got his full attention. He looked into my eyes and I conveyed something he needed—real guts.

All these incidents edged me a little closer toward being a better person. And there were more; many, many more.

I played soccer in junior high school. I returned a dirty hit that I had received. I kicked the shin of a girl as hard as I could. I was sorry even then. Her pain caused me to feel empathic pain; deep in my soul, I felt heavy and helpless. I carried that pain for days.

This incident taught me about the liberation that comes from forgiveness. Forgiving those who wronged me enabled my character to anchor into a deeper level of understanding.

I picked up some dull jewels that contained faint glimmers of hope. One incident caused me a lot of grief. *"For nothing is hidden that will not be made manifest, nor is anything secret that will not be known and come to light"* (Luke 8:17).

I used to walk over a mile to junior high school, sometimes in deep snow. One day, I was late, cold, hungry, and angry. I threw a hard snowball, and it hit a car's windshield. By the time the driver drove around the block to investigate, I was hiding inside a store, looking outside. No one had questioned me until right then. I relived this drastic event with a significant change: I was the driver in the car. The snowball came cracking into my view, and I felt devastating fear because I was driving fast without being able to see where I was going. As a consequence of this event, throughout life I was nervous while driving.

After that incident, I felt aimless and weary for days. In Heaven, as I examined such things, I could see that while I was on earth, I had unknowingly suffered repercussions for many of my actions. I analyzed my heart to find out how my life affected others. I received Heaven's reaction for each thought, every act.

Those closest to my life were more consciously receptive of my warm, honest intentions. I would never have imagined that unmentioned, good intentions actually brought great meaning into my Heavenly neighborhood. I witnessed my individual Love coming alive, little by little, one insignificant event at a time. I became a more vibrant, living soul.

For example, I could also see the long-term effects of my ignorant decisions. When I knew how to do good but did nothing, I lost momentum. My courage became carelessness. When I developed willpower without considering others, I was blinded by selfish arrogance, and this caused me to be self-destructive. Deliberate disregard to my honest premonitions numbed my spiritual sensibilities and callused my heart. Then, I would become confused when it came to making major decisions.

Being detached from my emotional and spiritual sensitivities caused me to find my desensitized place—the anguish of loneliness. I felt as if it were others who misunderstood me. I saw that many of my wrong actions caused me to endure lasting regret on earth, especially when I snubbed the very people that God had sent my way.

I also selected a brightly colored gemstone to enter; I studied the symmetrical patterns created by my energy fields. Each jewel carried many auras in living color. I could see clearly that my life fulfilled others when I listened to and followed my heart.

As I responded in faith to a little flicker of white *hope,* my faith turned my aura a transparent blue. When faith ascends into a higher order of understanding, humanity's love reflects a beautiful, luminous rose. The color of the translucent red rose of Sharon blending with blue faith is creation's handiwork. The color lilac blends with sky blue are the messages of divine living faith received through peaceful consciousness. Yellow gold reflects brightness and shimmers from spiritual gifts that blend and rearrange the colors. Green emerges through blues and yellows to establish new life. A white-blue rose becomes a glorious orchid violet that is supported by the White Light of angels.

I desired to see where I failed myself–this would be part of my spiritual evolution and my whole purpose for going to earth. This in turn led me to rationally recognize the difference in and the purpose for two kinds of loves.

It was very plain to see that basic, natural love is God showing me the nurturing process of life through creation so that I will accept that my pure Love is in alignment with the Creator. Physical, human love can reveal nature's order in the spiritual laws of creation. Being drawn by peace into the harmony of a comprehensive, all-encompassing Love, my light of truth gave me a orchid and White Light path to follow.

Many times, I had been subtly convinced, even compelled, into an obligatory love rather than trusting my spiritually inspired Love; I had accepted a wrong set of priorities. My conscience caused me to see that when I fell into an anxious mind-set, this made me more aware that I was displaced or detached from my peaceful, true higher self. Consequently, I realized that to recenter in the divine order of my soul and spirit, I would need to open my heart and receive insight from above.

I learned that our greatest goal in this lifetime is to willingly understand and be instrumental in divine Love. Human love is generous yet limited so that in our unfulfilled expectations of human love, we will reach for our Creator's divine Love.

In some instances, I was oblivious to my behavior and ignorantly followed others. When others depended on me for fulfillment, and when I was selfishly projecting my expectations onto them, I could plainly see that self-centered love resulted in disarray, anxiety, and confusion.

By thus reflecting on my life, I began to comprehend two different kinds of love, two spiritual paths of love both connected with my humanity. When I knowingly chose to disregard my heart's warnings, I not only became emotionally disconnected from my ancestral celestial family tree, Heaven's consciousness, but my actions also failed to help, and at the same time, hurt the spiritual growth of the people in my earthly life.

I observed as human love evolves into divine Love, a colorful, intelligent transformation brings alive a luminous aura of lilac.

Multicolors radiated eloquence, shining through many facets on many jewels. Pure Love protects us in its warm, sensational graces and encourages spiritual growth, *casting out all fear.*

Heaven's consciousness is radiating rainbow colors, providing an atmosphere of freedom in an environment of hope; it is an enlightened resonance of understanding in God's generosity. Many facets—windows—on my jewels shone brilliantly, reflecting that God's Love is the light of my rational, spiritual discernment that was always available. I discovered that as I accepted spiritual insight, my emotions responded intelligently, creating symmetrical growth patterns.

By trusting God's Love to arrange our circumstances justly, our consciousness accepts that little by little, we are learning to develop and sustain an ability to use good judgment. In divine Love, this evolves new spiritual life in living color into our family tree.

Free Will Decides

Decision of each finite heart will understand or resign
Cosmic forces create power, universal space in time
Choices compel response to receive and incline
We answer by willpower or withdraw to define
Words influence actions to fulfill or decline
To believe in truth, admit God's Love is divine
Accept our spiritual domain or, dismiss our grand design

11

Exploring Paradise

This lovely experience always causes me to smile; it brings to mind God's hilarious sense of humor. When I was a child, Curly was the mommy to at least two litters of darling baby goats. In Heaven, Curly's long, flowing, copper curls bounced as she danced around me in glee. She pranced around me to the tune of my love for her. The warm glow of my childhood love bloomed a place for my pet goat to live. When I saw Curly, we jumped and laughed together, reliving the thrills we shared when I was a little girl.

When I looked closer, I saw the shining love that dwelled in many pets as their loyal connections radiated the loving personalities from their earthly owners. Each one of Heaven's animals was special in its own way. Some little pets were resonating with a bond of love from their companions who were still on earth. Heaven's animals grew much larger than the animals from earth. They flew around, docile and friendly to everyone.

Inside my dome-shaped entryway, off to the side, gathered a small cluster of earth's pets. These precious friends patiently and diligently watch, waiting for their earthly owners to arrive. A little puppy had been following me since I entered. In Paradise, she had appeared in the near distance a few times. Several times, she had looked at me as if to say, "Do you remember me?" I could sense her temperament, and she felt mine because we were old friends. Her coat was shimmering, reflecting fluffy silver. It dawned on me that she was my childhood best friend, Sugar.

When I was about seven, Sugar was my sweet cocker spaniel. She still owned a tender place in my heart. My love for her was extremely strong, yet fragile. She was my whole world. I loved her without reservation.

As a child, I told my mother, "Sugar's dying caused my heart to be bursted (broken)."

As I relived her departure, I didn't call her to me. On earth, my last memory of her was very sad. I looked at her and she was sweet and happy. When we are both in Heaven, my heart will continue with our completion of one another. For now, Sugar will play with other loyal friends while she waits for me.

After my life review, omnipotence, or my extension of Spirit, became visible. We—by "we," I mean my gentle, strong extension of my magnificent Lord, my passion, and the gift of God's Spirit—beheld the rest of me in the form of my higher self—my Holy Spirit. All our thoughts were as one.

* * *

In Paradise, our interactions were clean, harmonized, and truly kindred. Our travel was directed by mental and telepathic focus. Everything from the sweetest little blooming bud to the most extravagant choir, all of Heaven, moves in the rhythm of Love.

We paused in an orchard where birds were creating a chorus. I was under a tree covered with soft, florescent, violet petals. The trunk rippled with character, including the leaves. All of Heaven's trees swayed to the melody. I noticed the color in the bark moved in tune with the birds' songs. The movements of the branches and the leaves added to the rhythm by clapping together. My attention was drawn to another tree in full swing with red birds singing a most lovely tune.

I learned the true meaning of worship as my enthusiasm bellowed out a whole-hearted adoration for our lives. New visions of God, permeated with colors, resonating incandescently within the music, created new realities for us to discover. As we dwelled there, we shared a very peaceful, musical arrangement—a concert of sorts.

The pulsing vibrato of angels and saints flowed in from the distance. The streets were clear-gold branches, swirling, intertwining high and low as grapevines.

Heaven's consciousness was continuous, harmonic sensations that vigorously moved through us. The Garden of Life filled us with splendor—plants, animals, everything was alive. The singing flowers' smiles sprung back in veneration of us. All of Heaven's creatures gave me the impression that our presence nurtured them.

I floated over a gorgeous meadow. Looking into the crystal-blue sky, I opened my mouth, and out of the center of my soul, an elegant, poetic concerto swirled from me, creating reflections of white and bright colors into the crystal-blue sky. The surrounding trees moved to the resonance of my heart. In response to my singing, the birds chimed in, too, as we created a new chorus together in joyful worship and thanksgiving. We shared our gratitude for eternal life. More birds chimed in as we made glorious music, adding volume and life to Heaven. Together we sang with the choir and the orchestra. We were all praising the Lord of creation. We harmonized in happiness for having the freedom to create our own personalities.

Faith?

I believe the future writes a melody
much sweeter than the past
I perceive there will be times of quandary
about the direction of our paths
Sometimes alone again
and then times to hold fast
When and where this hope does take us
and will it forever last
Give your melody to God believing
and your heart will show you how to share
Love this hope, this love to hope in me
and I will meet you there!

12

My Heavenly Neighbors

I went along the transparent gold streets above the river of living water to enter my neighborhood. I flew from a higher waterway into a group of little castles where my family lived.

Smiling faces silently shared, "We have been waiting on you."

I didn't stop to talk because I anticipated our coming together all at once. Through the ages, we all had ventured through the earthly realm together, helping and uplifting one another. Friends and relatives paused, giving me a genuine welcome. Familiar faces were on every side, gentle and kind, looking young, and with countenances projecting many memories, each one precious in a special way. We were all close friends venturing through life, carving out our destination in the Tree of Life.

Our dwelling places nestled closely together in our Love's auras of living colors that blended with Heaven's ambiance and appeared to be interconnected by similarity. Gentle music flowed through us and carried our thinking. The surfaces of every one of our domains shimmered with our souls' reflections, continuously moving with the music, blending colorful rays. Children's laughter echoed as they played in the open areas. Their giggles added to our homey feelings.

My mansion was unique to my personality, yet intertwined with the others; they were woven closely together, emerging from the branches and opening to the universe like petals of a water lily.

I saw in the distance more trees with bright, luscious fruits. Under the main expressway grew an elaborate arrangement of orchards for every neighborhood. The branches of the Tree of Life held the little palaces in place, like dome-shaped petals surrounding the heart of the flower.

Our Heavenly homes were nicely styled over transparent, gold streets that branched out into clusters of neighborhoods. My neighbor's home was one continuous branch that swirled over valleys, hills, and gardens. All the lovely mansions were growing from the same river of life. Pure, sweet, flowing, musical water came down from the throne. The foundation under the stairs leading up to the entrance of my dwelling was embedded with living stones, little nuggets, or living seeds. These growing, glistening gems sparkled around the base of my home.

My better half and I slowly floated into the center room, entering through a shimmering, yellow area like a solarium. We passed by cheering flowers that were hanging out of box windows, welcoming us. I felt cuddled and snug, as if in a huge, warm comforter after a cool shower.

My home was delicately and precisely crafted by my good intentions, fairly small but pretty and perfect. With my tranquility anchored, I found the seat of my soul. I rested in contemplation; now I was to discover the vast nature of my character. The walls were soft, like rose petals. The rooms were round with high ceilings. The doors and windows were openings with no drawstrings. One wall blended in three shades that reflected life and changed color, the way that a sunset does. We all viewed the glorious garden from our balconies, which overlooked breathtaking waterfalls.

In my first walk-through, I looked for a kitchen, bathroom, bedroom, and a private area but didn't find any. There was no living room, either. My probing mind received answers.

For example, "Where is the place to gather others together in here?"

The answer was specific and came with visions of a meeting place. I was shown a vision of the center garden. My attention was drawn to a delightful arrangement of delicious foods, which we grew and shared together in the Garden of Life. I looked out the back window at a panoramic view. Fountains and springing waterfalls were translucent, bursting with life. Massive varieties of multicolored fruit bloomed like jewels for us to share in our family reunions.

Against one of the walls there was a golden trumpet that must have been placed there by one of my angels. I carefully put it to my mouth and gently blew. My breath increased the symphony's tempo as my tone rippled the announcement of my homecoming.

The horn propelled my consciousness, my individual prism, in living color. My triumphant tune rang incrementally throughout my neighborhood. Other residents in my hierarchy felt my announcement. I received their uplifting reaction. Our greetings came in musical reflections of joy.

The center room had winding stairs that led to a private, secret place—an enormous window that opened into the divine order of our cosmos. Light orbs are glowing balls of White Light reflecting colors of the rainbow. The colors convey conversations. Huge light beings, some bigger than others, show expressive thoughts toward others. These stars emanated the intelligence of the celestial sons and flowed in perfection and coordination. In my highest communion with my Lord, I viewed creation's infinity and saw multiple light bodies that appeared to be stars, planets or, galaxies actively communicating. Each light orb's disposition was moved by Heaven's consciousness throughout the universe. All were perfectly situated in Love's dimensions and bonded together in their divine authority. My thoughts blended with Heaven's consciousness.

I had an inherent feeling that my soul was in spiritual interaction within my dimension of evolved consciousnesses and that I was peering into my destiny's passageways—my future. There shone many celestial trees that spread out, interwoven like galaxies, moving within the mind of God. As I stargazed in amusement, within me I felt absorbed by their joyful sensations. I knew that creation was moved by my every thought as my intuition resonated within the course of the pure consciousness of the Creator. My life is eternally one in my spiritual relationship; my realizations danced in the light, the glory of Heaven's cosmos.

Each little palace in my neighborhood was adorned with lookout towers on the rooftops. These towers were where the depth of our soul interconnected in smooth discourse with Heaven's consciousness.

We built our upper rooms when our free will's choices were in synch with our individual Holy Spirit. The light of God's Love helps us understand our eternal value in our self-discovery.

As I peeked into infinity, my spirit rushed forward in adoration as I experienced perfect unity with enormously massive, twirling, streaming starlike consciousnesses. My spiritual emotions were caught up in everlasting Love. My understanding of life became all-knowing to the extent of my ability to blend. I was telepathically communicating with intelligent, celestial sons, brilliant planets of God's own children. My perspective expanded from simply enjoying Heaven's persuasions into adoration of the author of my soul.

We are precious stars and jewels in the divine order of infinity. My self-discovery was in my "entanglement" with the living universe. My mind harmonized with many precious jewels. I am in God's collaborative effort to evolve life.

I became aware I was in communion with our Lord's closest friends, permeating antennas, gleaming light bodies, living stars shining blissfully, transferring pure consciousness with one another. Each jewel center pulsated coherently in harmonic music. The colorful, blooming orbs of glowing consciousness made me rejoice.

"The birth of Christ brought a bright and morning star. When they saw the star, they rejoiced exceedingly with great joy" (Matthew 2:10).

I found my location and my rhythm. Each moment was new; I was new. I was never one to search the skies for Solomon's great secrets or the key to Jacob's ladder. My spirit is one with my Creator's wisdom, unfolding my life's purpose one pulse at a time.

My consciousness discovered Love's divine pure authority as I delved into deep space. My secret place within the Most High is my ultimate communion. The White Light of Creator Lord's omniscience resonates divine Love holding us up in our universe.

By entering and blending in unity, all the collective consciousnesses on earth and throughout Heaven created a symphony, bringing more life into creation. In adoration and true worship, our righteous Lord enlightened us in the essence of pure Love. We're channeled into dimensional currents through waves of light.

In a deep, sweet, settled peace springing forth from fountains of enthusiasm, we can shout the good news from the rooftops. My private realm in my sacred upper room rested neatly on a branch of living water.

All of our little castles were designed to give our hearts an ability to open up like a blooming flower to experience oneness with creation. My being one with infinity, I felt as though I was in the White Light of God's eyes holding the keys of timelessness to the kingdom of Heaven.

In the white fire of our Lord's breath, my life flowed with the heart of infinity. My soul joined the army of the archangels. God's celestial family is the network in the river of everlasting life. Love is a glorious arrangement of saints and angels. By blending into the nature of each variety, we become their joy of life, creating a fresh arrangement in an ongoing orchestra.

We built our homes in Paradise by dwelling in the spirit of wisdom. *"Every good and perfect gift is from above, coming down from the Father of lights with whom there is no variation or shadow of change"* (James 1:17).

I will always be free to go to my upper room with my Father's best friends to see my destiny's future options.

Deep Love

Deep within my inner soul are memories never told
Of sorrow and joy left behind
In my consciousness, true Love surfaces bringing
Joy and peace to my mind
As I grow in meditation, I discover revelation
Within me is God's grand design
Finding new light within, some say, I am born again
I know Heaven's Love is mine
In God's infinite wisdom, I find realizations
Unfolding within me the divine
A new purpose for living, true Love is giving
Within each other's joy when we find
Heaven has true pleasure, in finding a treasure
Within our hearts when we are kind
Loving Heaven's bliss, is our original purpose
While on earth we are refined
In true Love divine, we transcend space and time
Through death, we reign with Heaven's kind
Created to grow, given more Love to sow
We are given a new name and signed

13

Time Traveling: Levels of Heaven

I anticipated further time traveling with my celestial friends. Heaven was very busy, responding to the prayers from earth. Bursting with elation, I was thrilled with my new-found depth of clarity. I pursued the truth about life. My Holy Spirit revealed the way to another area. We traveled through comforting black space up into another timeless level into a more finely tuned, smoother intelligence.

We went through a portal away from Paradise into a dark, clean vortex that propelled us into dimensional paths in the crown of God's mind, all the while evolving and sharing our Creator's living universe. We were beaming in tranquility, swirling in celestial traffic. I traveled with messengers—symmetrical light bodies coming toward me and following behind.

We ventured between levels of Heaven in currents and moved about very liberally, shining in the darkness and guided by the enlightenment of our own radiance; our grace was flowing from our souls' revelations; we were traveling in waves of Love's divine order. All around us, it appeared as condensed as the Milky Way looks in pictures.

On occasion, we embraced in passing, geometrically fused with one another, freely sharing our gifts. We communicated in living color, growing new antennas, reaching into new regions of light, interweaving with one another, bestowing blessings as we went forward. Upon contact, we activated one another's potential, charging and increasing our mutual momentum.

As we passed through each other, we merged and absorbed one another's personas. We infused one another with our spiritual awareness, our fires of truth bearing witness through our centrifugal forces permeating from our souls. By sharing an astonishing exchange of our own individual, glorious realities, we enriched one another. Through our communion, we grew in the excellence of God's immense qualities and character by embracing one another and imparting our gifts and virtues.

As we ventured through the King's passageways in pure blackness, while in light orb formation, our development was expanding. Huge, spinning, pulsating flowers—stunning, sensational, and glimmering—and colorful aromas fulfilled one another with their countenances; their consciousnesses were their own wonderful image of God.

Everyone that I "felt," I received back an impression of his or her consciousness. We glowed like geometrically perfect light blooms.

Engaging in the Creator's qualities was beyond any pleasure and the most euphoric sensation that I had ever known. *We were forming streams of lights, creating veins reaching to find the flow of clean blood.* Our willpower created antennas—Love antennas were coming out of our hearts. We spiritually shared the depth of our Love's gifts in reflections of new colors. This expanded my concentration.

I felt a glorious, sobering, genuine gratitude for being among God's beloved friends. An overwhelming sweet peace seized my heart with the extreme assurance of being Loved and being intricately involved with creation.

Each one of us, a jewel, held a uniquely definite, majestic, interesting composition. Our own personas were treasures and reflections of Love.

I continued to be very talkative, reflecting luminous thoughts as I observed a lot of traffic going in both directions. *We were transported, propelled by spiritual stamina and carried by a current in God's mind, a living pulsation in these brain waves.* The closer we came to the center of creation, the greater God's immensity arose in all of us.

We bathed in this solemn inner knowing of our spirits taking shape. While bringing our exhilarating pleasures in Love's nurturing intimacy, we were adding to the progression of creation.

As we traveled, the closer we were to the Most High, the stronger and more vividly we exchanged our spiritual insights. Some of us were of a much more complex composition, like multiple flavors in one delicious bite. Everyone who made contact shared individual feelings and emotions by merging or simply touching.

Between Paradise and the Most High, our personas propelled us in harmonious, symmetrically awe-inspiring colors; some were greater in spiritual wisdom. In passing, our luminous messages incited exciting vital information. Our sizes, colors, and sensations varied by reflections of our spiritual growth. Fluctuating in our growth, we were all being finely tuned for extended travel in the tidal waves of the universe.

I wasn't as large or as bursting with strength or as bright as most of the others. My symmetrical continuity was petite among very full and graciously thrilling formations. My center fused when I symmetrically aligned, wheel within wheels, as we telepathically shared our souls. I beheld large, highly decorated, endowed beings of illuminating consciousnesses, along with the smaller ones, including me. We communicated by blending with each other, creating new essences. In this way, we were also intensifying our relationship with God. Bestowing our signatures into the depth of one another's souls by a center fusion, we hugged as we glided through one another.

I received transfusions that strengthened my inner knowledge of the multidimensional order of our Creator's compassionate life. In passing, we changed one another's lives. Our gifts, in imagery and clarity, were applications for the rest of our eternal lives.

I desired to focus on the vivacious, larger-than-my-life, spectacular beings. I tried to go into their enlightened consciousness to merge but could not. I had the impression that I needed more spiritual muscle, which is precisely why I chose to live on earth. With all my strength, I could muster only a certain amount of "stamina," or as we call it on earth—faith. With all my confidence and knowledge of God that I had attained, even then my courageous soul was small among great personalities.

In my quest for life's answers, my eyes were opened to see that according to our original lineages, we all derived from specific locations, building our own identity. Like a seed emerges to form a plant to face the sun, predestined to be a particular color and size, we, too will become fully featured.

God is tempering us, highlighting us in a harmonious sequence of events. Love's reigning generosity far exceeds our furthest imagination. Our own constitution of the God gene tenderly faces the light. We are all evolving, becoming alive in new spiritual awareness as our relationship and receptivity of Love expands.

Saturated in pure virtue, flowing in the genius of God's sacred vision for mankind, I felt compelled to make a decision. In my perpetual motion in Love's everlasting river of life, I will fulfill my life's purpose as my soul evolves into God's intelligent design.

Our countenances whirled as multicolored, kaleidoscopic, multifaceted wheels. We were creating new patterns of Love, advancing God's precious investments. We brightly infused one another with our colorful auras of truth as we were being beautified in an array of spectacular enlightenment. Our soul's prism imprinted our signatures that forever bonded in one another's Book of Life.

I was less developed than most. There were many more advanced giants that were in precision brilliancy with God. They were endowed with a greater sensitivity to omniscience. Multidimensional Love from their countenances gracefully spread out genius reflections. Planets permeating consciousness as pleasantly graceful fragrances were as swirling rainbows, blessing everyone in their environment.

I felt fortunate just to see into these dimensions. I could sense that their Love was beyond my ability to respond. I was unable to get close to some of the gigantic ones, farther out as distant stars operating in a greater clarity. Maybe they were Joshua, Job, and Enoch, being held in their ancestral garden of life by archangels from God's beloved hierarchy. When certain ones came close, they caused unparalleled sensations. Maybe these were the biblical personalities that I identified with as I read the Scripture—Isaiah, King David, Solomon, or Saint John.

I thought, "We are flowing in the pulse of creation, traveling within the main thoroughfare between two dimensions of infinity in the Creator's excellence."

When I came upon greatly endowed beings or intelligent stars, I experienced sensational, overwhelming thrills of excitement equivalent to their intelligences. As their glowing orbs shined on me, the slightest touch radiated through me. A new enthusiasm ignited me with dimensional fields of Love's magnitude, a righteousness that I could never understand enough to express from my mortal mind. I found the glory in Heaven's spiritual expansion process of consciousness most fulfilling.

Their dignity and character provided me more meaning about the purpose of spiritual evolution and an inner knowledge of God's everlasting brilliance that was evolving us with gentle kindness. I knew that all of Heaven existed by spiritual relationships. Impressed deeply and eternally, bonded in deep Love, I will never be the same.

You Light Up My Life

Beams of amusement gleam through our lives
Our heart is transparent; we are not in disguise
Our life is peaceful within comprehensive ties
Our beautiful relation as omnipotence guides
Cognitive sparks of hope cause us to realize
Our connection we know, no longer surmise
Our personal feelings of dimensional size
Embrace one essence in one another's lives
In our relationships, we evolve to new highs

14

Heaven Is Orchestrated by Music

Music orchestrates Heaven's activity. As I arrived in the throne area, I noticed we all wore soft, white luminous robes radiating our signatures from our prisms, blending in vibrant color and melody. In this dimension, God's celestial giant sons were bodies of White Light. I was thrilled with their joy as they were creating exclusive plans.

I stood in wonderment and thought to myself, "Maybe they are evolving into lords to rule over their universes."

Their high spirits and extreme joy caused me to laugh out loud in heightened pleasure. We stood on the edge of Heaven's immaculate plateau, discovering creation, blending our consciousnesses with Heaven's greatest musicians and architects.

I thought, "I must be standing in the heart of the Lord of creation, in the pulse that hammers out glorious messages through volumes of virtuous music."

I stood in awe, seeing how God breathed Love into creation. New life was taking shape, generated from omniscient sounds that resonated from archangels and celestial bodies. Volumes of intelligent Love were shaping in living color the formations and orchestrating the structured arrangements that decorated the sky. Every evolved soul permeated a unique essence in an elaborate expression of joy.

Luke said: "If then your whole body is full of light, having no part dark, it will be wholly bright, as when a lamp with its rays gives light" (Luke 11:36).

Heaven's most resourcefully adorned celestial sons, crowned with brilliant jewels, had radiantly lighted heads. They were in synch with the creative music that gushed from our Creator's throne. God's sons continuously shared hilarious laughter as they articulated creation. These enormous angels or light beings emanated telepathic messages in living color and precision timing with the choir. Their countenances, bonded together in pure Love, projected images along with conveyances of humorous, joyful jesters.

I plunged into their spiritual flow in the thought process with Heaven's royals. The heart of the Tree of Life was brimming with fruit of the spirit. Through the sky, elegance rang from high in the distance. My heart's rhythm flowed with the melodies.

Heaven's choir was high above the orchestra, positioned in our Creator's deity; divine order was orchestrating new life. The graceful blending of voices with instruments rang throughout. The orchestras were revolving. While one group played, another group gathered to play. Saints and loved ones, whose prayers were in the process of being answered, lined up in position, waiting for their turn in this revolving choir. I remember the boundless wonder I felt as they exchanged places without missing a beat.

I believed that some of the musicians were saints from earth and some were celestial sons and daughters of God. Gifted saints along with many friends from earth grew up nurturing their loved ones while refining their musical gifts. Now in Heaven's choir, their kind hearts were nurturing their family tree in Heaven's music, contributing their unique enthusiasm. The birds and the flowers added their supportive presence; every living creature directed joyful adoration toward the Most High.

From earth, loving intentions added richness to Heaven. According to the way people on earth respond to their spiritual family, our Creator transforms their intentions into visual manifestations. Every faithful intention changes the course of nature by the power of the spoken word in earth's space, creating time in God's pure continuum through the Holy Spirit. Streaming virtues from earth blended in, weaving musical arrangements into their personal Heavenly neighborhoods. Humble prayers and sweet, little heartfelt intentions generate fresh, whirling Love that gushes throughout Heaven.

The flowing, crystal-clear waterway carries the answers to the prayers. There is a continual response from the family lineage into their own domain to nurture the advancement of their Loved ones on earth.

Intuitively answered prayers to the faithful people on earth who accept the peace that surpasses worldly understanding opens the windows of Heaven. Mighty winds surge, lifting our tempo, sharing the magnificence of the Creator. God's messengers of White Light arise into living stars that cruise higher realms. Our faithful prayers transcend human energy fields to evolving, spiritual consciousness, growing formations and expanding our universe.

Celestial royal armies of light adorned Heaven as living jewels wondrously moved in synchronization in the crown of glory. "Is there any number to his armies? Upon whom does his light not arise?" (Job 25:3).

Far above me, God's friends were in discussion, telepathically projecting images to one another as they proposed new creative designs, fortifying the living quarters for new believers. Celestial sons beamed holographic thoughts, giving descriptions to Heaven's architects. In perfect color, music, and imagery, I was caught up in the realm of God's Love. I began digesting how pure consciousness is the spiritual evolution that expands the universe. God's breath of life, full of living wisdom, is guiding our consciousness and spiritually fulfilling our intelligent design. God's grace is permeating the light of Love, transforming earthly matter into radiant friends.

Daniel says: "At this time shall arise Michael, the great prince who has charge of your people. And there shall be a time of trouble such as never has been since there was a nation (family) since that time (cycle). But, at that time your people shall be delivered (shine away the darkness), everyone whose name (identity) shall be found written (rooted and grounded in the Book of Life) in the book (the Garden of Life)" (Daniel 12:1).

Our Lord's will moves through Heavenly family trees. The earth's spiritual support systems are Heavenly bodies sharing the pulse of creation, progressively evolving within this complex composition of divine intelligence. Creation in spirit is continually progressing and growing toward perfection in the everlasting river of change.

The dazzling musicians' tempo, flowing in precise rhythm, intensified my sensitivities. Heaven's plush aristocrats took turns interacting in the process of creation. New, believing souls blended in musical colors of lightning in the expansion of Heaven—God's firmament. We were all excelling into intimate, trustworthy friends, bonded in perfect balance. All of Heaven's consciousnesses are the everlasting life that through our spiritual evolution orchestrates new realities within us.

Our spiritual intelligence is our own soul's glow of grace bringing forth new life. Our eternal life perpetually expands Heaven's consciousness in God's Holy Spirit. Much like the sunlight changes the course of nature, the acceleration of our Love is the evolution of spirit in the everlasting river of life. "The Heavens declare the glory of God; and the firmament (expansion of the Heavens) show his handiwork" (Psalms 19:1).

From earth's root system of the celestial Tree of Life, branches stretch up to revolving, glowing, humming planets. There were smaller ones, wonderful light orbs, musically blossoming over the Garden of Life. Nobility resonated through highly evolved saints, revealing glorious graces.

Gabriel's angels are the voice of reason in concert with Michael's armies. Offspring from the King of Wisdom reign in dignity and eloquence. Clearly visible, countless royally exquisite, celestial organizations of reigning dignitaries stabilize our living universe. The mind of God is a widespread information network of creative spiritual consciousness (Matthew 13:47).

This same light is healing Love through the laws of creation, revealed through relationships within every trusting heart.

I renewed my commitment to Heaven's wealth. "Now unto the King eternal, immortal, invisible, the only wise God, be honor and glory forever and ever, Amen" (1 Timothy 1:17).

A Jewel

May your days be filled with wonder
And your heart be filled with bliss
Free yourself in boundless laughter
Absorb your spirit's exquisiteness
Explore life, your value is without measure
Time will tell you are God's saved treasure
A fresh outlook, a sweet pleasure
In thankfulness, in love for life
Throw the sky a kiss

15

Sometimes We Call Them Saints

We entered into another realm in Heaven where believers built buildings by being receptive to their higher spiritual selves, their Holy Spirit. First born in the spirit, spiritual evolution continually adapts to God's wisdom in the everlasting river of life. Heaven was created first, and by true Love, spiritual life resumes.

God's very own character draws and aligns with certain people, preparing them for lives of devotion. Within the lineages of mortal humans, our Lord brought forth a splendid resolution to purify, to bring into perfection, to endear with high excellence in order for us to share an undeniable presence with the higher ranks in Heavenly places—our hierarchy.

In the resilience of Love through humanity, pure consciousness came through Gabriel to Mary, the mother of Jesus. Prophetic words that aligned with well-advanced, noble saints are now available to all who have an ear to hear them. In our willing character, we, too develop courage to excel in fulfilling our purpose. Our life's little choices edify the Love in one another, invigorating Heaven. As we walk in the light of our Holy Spirit, we, too become responsive in the flow of our reigning Lord (Psalms 89:15).

In Heaven's domain, some devout saints served to guide their followers. In the Holy Spirit, saints lived disciplined lives that helped lead their followers, even the ones who did not comprehend that they were living through their spiritually evolved reasoning. Sometimes, we call saints the believers who, by free choice, wholeheartedly dedicated their lives' purpose to becoming an example of pure Love. Through their willingness to follow a life of devotion, as requested of our Lord, they entered into sainthood. Their Holy Spirits devised their way, implementing their desires to become one with the Lord of creation, bringing balance to those in their midst.

God receives all true spiritual devotion that serves humanity for the common spiritual good. Loving, nurturing, and preserving life in support of divine order makes way for the light of grace to shine, enabling a comprehensive adherence to the Holy Spirit. All well-advanced, noble saints strengthen Heaven's deity.

Many saints, predestined to become trailblazers on the high road of God's consciousness, never received earthly saint notoriety, but their righteousness added to and increased the magnitude of Heaven. Some precious, unknown saints' consciousnesses carved psychological and spiritual paths leading toward enlightenment before and after the life of Christ.

Noble souls were bright diadems, some placed in the crown of our Lord's reigning, living universe in Heaven's structure. Many saints on earth were protected by the light of their hierarchy but were never honored for their contributions. Their habitats, built by disciplined lives, provided their celestial family tree root systems that held strong branches on the Tree of Life, bearing an array of Lovely fruits.

Heaven is adorned with wonderful, intelligent jewels. Love is growing seedpods in perfect symmetrical decorations—the fruit of the spirit. Spiritual life continually reveals interesting wisdom, strengthening our interconnectedness within our Heavenly arrangements.

The saints' virtues were the knowledge that grew into spiritual continuity. God's expressive will is cultivated in spiritual consciousness and is continually creating. Heaven's consciousness radiated in the nobility and colored their individuality, distinguishing their identity. For every small sacrifice, there was a higher commission and reward.

A saint's dwelling place towered over his or her Garden of Life, reflecting elegant arrays of lighted aromas flowering in sensational, musical chimes. They built plush neighborhoods with celestial aristocrats, distinctive in their peace and soundness in relationship of God's Love.

As we left that area, I noticed soft clouds gathered outside some of the saints' open neighborhoods. There, sleeping people hovered together in quiet clouds, on the outskirts of Paradise, next to their saints' tenancies—fluffy, sleeping souls.

I understood that many people lived lives believing only in the love of their human relationships. In their mortal lives, they loved the visions of their saints.

Our Lord's great compassion and perfection in justice enriches all who choose true spiritual devotion. (All earth's religions that accept rational thought agree with the law of reciprocity.) The saints gave of their lives, and they received accordingly. We all reap what we sow; life gives back according to all it is given.

Saints flow through the living water (just as you and I) all through the ages into maturity. I thought, "Saints and sleeping souls will awaken in response to the wonders of God's purpose in their grand design."

As I went past the clouds of spiritually asleep people, I found that I was hovering near a ceiling, invisible in a crowded room where hundreds or maybe even thousands of priests sat chanting the rosary below me. I assumed these, too were sleeping souls.

There was a sea of priests as far as I could see. They sat sanctimoniously close to one another, seemingly fully satisfied, in formal black robes and white collars. All in unity and very somber, they repeated the Lord's Prayer. They were fairly calm and studious and trancelike, content in their religious conformity. They carefully articulated each decade. They sat as though they were resting in wait of their next ordinance.

I looked around as if to learn what was going on. I had never heard the rosary. About that instant, their chant led them to the Lord's Prayer. The Lord's Prayer carried words or cognitive imagery in its waves of living water flowing throughout Heaven. I opened my mouth and in my new-found wisdom began to envision what these words meant as I spoke along with them. Still invisible to them, I began chanting with them, acknowledging the meaning of each word. I knew the Lord's Prayer very well although I didn't repeat it as though I were following the King James version. The spirit of God filled my mouth with expanded understanding. I prayed from my heart, sensational feelings resonating along with rational meaning with clarity in new phrases.

"Omnipotent Holy Spirit, give me new life in my daily courage so I may understand gratitude and take great pleasure in knowing the truth about who I am in you."

The priests, who were thirsty for living water, looked up. They responded to the light from above. Their angels over them incited their reactions. My words rained into beloved priests' hearts, getting their full attention.

Their prayers, along with the prayers of their loved ones, had mounted like rain clouds over their heads. Through the years, the faith in prayers coagulated brightly over them. New light, which gave them spiritual vision to see their inheritance archived through the years, formed clouds that dropped on them like a blast from the past. God's breath of living water rained into their hearts.

Easily accepting their Heavenly families' consciousnesses within their same nationalities, tongue, and creed, words of life meant for only them ignited their comprehension. Lighted, individually designed truth, especially from people who Loved them, brought new meaning into their self-value.

In Heaven's timeless dimension, words of life penetrated their souls. Spiritual faith became as pure rainwater on a thirsty garden and filled their open hearts to overflowing. Some more somber faces began to light up by accepting their higher divine reasoning in their Heavenly Holy Spirit. This caused a few to laugh out loud. "Whoever believes in me," as the Scriptures has said, "Out of his belly will flow rivers of living water " (John 7:38).

I saw the effectiveness of my little willing heart.

There sparked a fresh, new pulse that began to move in harmony with Heaven's music, bringing into their consciousness new revelations.

Glorious words of thanksgiving flooded in from their own family and friends. More somber faces began to be enlivened. Each priest, delicately designed by the touch of God's breath, will accept his liberation by shedding his black robes as a butterfly sheds its cocoon. In Heaven, all will receive the fruit of their spiritual labors as their virtual lives ascend into the image and character of God.

Growing in Grace

To live by grace in peace rejoice
Now strength within; a silent voice
To walk in the light is our solemn choice
In humility we are transparent
Preserved by angels Loving spirit
In sacred hope, God's Love revealed
Pure wisdom shows us we are healed
Our fellowship in grace divine
Heaven's Love is yours and mine
Together, we live in peace
We are the Lord's masterpiece

16

Beginning with Heaven

In the beginning, God created Heaven. In Heaven, there are no barriers to limit our understanding. In Heaven, my adaptability was much greater as we time traveled. Moving through levels of Heaven was much like thinking complex and always changing subjects. I believe that my passion grew to understand the purpose of life on earth. In Heaven, all my questions were continually and precisely answered. On earth, some Scriptures taught me, all eternal life was made first in Heaven and preordained to be influential throughout eternity (Proverbs 8:22-31).

My inquiries are the same as each and every truth seeker. While my soul receives understanding from my omnipotent teacher, I learn to listen to my heart's wisdom. All life exists to reach perfection; to be in one with God's spirit throughout creation. In Heaven's consciousness, my life's unanswered mysteries demanded answers. I desired to find the missing pieces hidden or left out of the Good Book.

"When and where was my soul born?

"Why was I on earth?"

"Why is there so much suffering on earth?"

My spirit responded to my questions in divine order, glorious and alive as everyone is perfectly graced in Paradise. The throne is in the center position, the Tree of Life. Water flows through Heaven's golden, transparent streets, branching throughout and over the sanctuaries of the Garden of Life. The streets lead to lively neighborhoods where families dwell.

Just as there are various kinds of plants and animals on earth, there is an immense variety in Heaven's domain. Creation's mysterious laws are spiritually revealed as we cocreate our destinies. *"Truly, truly, I say to you, we speak of what we know, and bear witness to what we have seen, but you do not receive (connect with) our testimony. If I told you earthly things, and you do not believe, how can you believe, if I tell you of Heavenly things?"* (John 3:11–12).

All experiences in Heaven are unique and exceptional. This kept me rooted in the present and in suspense while discovering more about my future purpose.

We went through branching passageways far back in the past, through time portals or dimensions that changed our countenances and comprehension. Our travel was directed by my seeking the truth about earth life. It felt structured, as though we were in God's brain, interacting with eminent, lighted intelligences, enormous orbs that looked like swirling planets. Some channels of life branched into Paradise, and others branched into what I understood were a vortex between levels of Heaven.

In hindsight, the inside of Heaven's creative flow was as the structure of an atom that can be understood only by its parts. An atom acts much like our universe, which is redefined through time, changing the course of nature. A cell's nucleus's chromosomes divide according to its genes in adaptation with its environment. God's living spirit, being one living system of regal cooperation, brings creation alive much the same way.

Our Holy Spirit's omnipotent light shines into our human soul to help guide our development. We, too evolve according to the progression and character of our soul's expression, which is innately similar to our spiritual families.

As I ventured closer to where I was ultimately heading, I had a sense of nearing home. My environment became more familiar. Everything felt like me, very intrinsic to my nature. The whole area exuded with feelings of my character.

I knew this area very well. My overall reality became settled, as though I were visiting a childhood park where I had spent many hours in my tender years. I found my fundamental boundaries, the heart of my intelligence. This is the place where my intellect found my senses; the wall where I first saw the light of Heaven and discovered life's waves that brought forth new life in me; here was my original domain.

Heaven is a timeless manifold of emerging dimensions continually unfolding and multiplying new life. God is breathing living sounds of music throughout. The Father of Light is instilling new and living ways in countless multifaceted relationships and enabling his offspring to be creative. The joy of life arises already evolved in the discovery of expanded reasoning. All consciousnesses are created to be intelligently instrumental and are uniquely developing all along the way.

My original point of view was facing me.

"I originated from precisely here," I thought.

I was looking at the wall where I had come from. My passion was driving me to discover these most sought-after answers, taking me to my origin. When I turned around and placed the seat of my soul into my exact location, it all dawned on me.

I saw Heaven from the vantage point of where I first became alive. Before I knew that I was a living soul or an organism, an embryo, or a moving entity, I was very small, maybe the size of an atom. I grew along with my domain in the structure of God's dignity. From my vantage point, Heaven was all too familiar as I peered into my past. This was where I began resonating with my environment. Before I developed, before I was an I or a me, as I am now in Heaven, I originated from this lovely place. My true beginning, the life within my consciousness, my soul was made in Heaven.

In the beginning, God created Heaven where I received my first breath of fresh life. I believe that creation moves by God's Love to perfect consciousness, creating universes to evolve in pure, divine relationships.

A solemn truth rested in my whole existence that forever changed my paradigm. Before I had a free will or opened my heart to a living conscience, I was a very small increment on the inside surface of a branch of Heaven. My family emerged out of the Tree of Life.

I was stationed in the region where rivers of living water flowed past me. The breath of God caused the water to glisten. Before me in colors that moved with the music, rainbows like prisms were glowing from enlightened souls that passed through. Their virtuous Love enhanced the origin of my spiritual journey as the water channeled in two directions in front of me. The colors moved with the music as the river of living water carried intelligent souls in its streams.

Eventually, light's frequencies in Heaven's music harmonized with me. The stanzas of living, celestial beings flowing past me, glowing, resonating new realms brought forth new life within me. I began springing into a more cognitive reaction in adaptation from my Creator.

I paused and looked in the distance and relived the season and place where I derived from. In my beginning, I grew from an atom, a seed, a fractal, a larva; just a little part of the wall.

I began traveling with Heaven's life in celestial growth. Heaven is alive, and every living bit within it is continuously refining new life, bringing beautification into Love's perfection. I was a tiny living tidbit of the Tree of Life in Heaven's consciousness.

I awakened to our original rhythm and blues in the sound of music inside our crystal-blue formation. I began to wonder about the rest of Heaven, our feelings came alive. I began to hear a deeper melody that influenced me into moving. The music off in the distance penetrated my senses with a sequence of intriguing flavors. I began to respond in synch with the angel's harmonic tones. I connected with the rhythm in Heaven's consciousness and began a new discourse.

The whole wall attentively and collectively began reverberating slightly. In amplified pure sound, our place peaceful wall melted like a huge glacier. Everyone of us within the area where I originated, fell into the streaming river of souls in Heaven's Tree of Life. Eventually, we were flowing in a vein through the portals of God's own heart. We were all in an ocean of Love that was nurturing us as we were moving along in the river of eternal souls. I shared an intrinsic connection with my family as each us began life's new voyage.

Like fruit falling into the light of life, we merged into a definite direction while assuming our individuality. We no longer occupied a tiny place inside of a branch. Still alive and coherent, I relived my reformation. Although we harmonized with the majestic choir, each one of us became individual essences. We were small increments of life that would eventually arise into celestial beings and commune according to the characters of our intelligent designs. As destiny would have it, like a seed in the river of everlasting life, we will arise together.

We were all blending into our intended environments. Each one of us took on a different form. We were in increments, yet continued to be familiar with the origins of one another as we moved forward in spirit. Our lives will spiritually grow within the light of our Holy higher selves.

I thought, "My Heavenly family and I first began our lives' quest from right here."

We have been intrinsically connected since our inception. Creation's clock in the cycle of our lives moves by our consciences. As we adapted to our oneness in everlasting Love of Heaven, we understood that our spirit was created in God's image. Our adaptability increased our creativeness to a brighter level to bless the Lord.

It seemed logical to me that our eternal souls shall arise as stars in glory and form our own planetary systems.

As children, we began to understand that we were growing by the vitality of the saints. Everyone became individuals in various ways. We were affected by our circumstances and responded to the nurturing of one another accordingly.

Bonded together in the Love of God, we will eventually mature and be moved by compassion toward the less fortunate that God has placed in our midst.

The season came when I became aware that we had a hierarchy of saints whose prisms of Love were much more indelible and pronounced. The "noble saints," as we sometimes called them, lived transparent lives, accentuating the attributes in one another. I, too was given life to mature and will bring out the best in others along the way.

"I, too will bear fruit."

As I gleaned from the saints, I, too am predestined to advance to become innately harmonious with God in our universe.

First, I will receive my free will in my gift of life and will be blessed with a unique soul to develop my own Love for life. Created in Heaven, I decided to be born on earth. My free choice on earth enabled me to grow in divine Love. My Love will grow so I may share the gift of eternal life. God's will through creation is an everlasting, methodical, spiritual, and eminent wonder, continually evolving for the perfection of spirit. My connection to my spiritual family will always be closely knit. We nurture one another, most of the time unaware of our involvement.

My Holy, omnipotent, spiritual extension continued to answer my questions.

"Why is there so much suffering on Earth?"

There are interdimensional, terrestrial dark entities inhabiting the earth; they are the fallen ones who once received the nurturing of the Lord then endeavored to use the light of their Creator's wisdom to draw to themselves Heaven's possession. Since they detached, they are unable to comprehend moral justice. No longer connected to their original domain, they have fallen into disharmony. They are lost in soulless darkness; degenerating in fear, they cannot understand divine order.

The Bible refers to them as gods, including, "The god of this world has blinded the minds of the unbelievers to keep them from seeing the light of the gospel of the glory of Christ (the anointed light) who is the image of God" (2 Corinthians 4:4).

Other principalities who have power over many worldly leaders proclaim that humanity alone possesses the crown of creation. Detached, they lack adaptability and cannot understand true Love. They align only with earth's dark interdimensional, spiritual terrestrials and are earthbound through cycles in history. Degraded into destructive creatures, their battle cry is warfare to attain power over earth's consciousnesses.

Parasites only depend on the consumption of the planet's native resources. Spiritually impoverished humanity, bound in religious formations, has forgotten to seek truth, knowledge, wisdom, and Love. Resisting knowledge to gain authority and popularity, humanity depends on illogical ideas coming from many imposters and false leaders making truths into lies, virtues into untruths, to further man-made disciplines.

Spiritually blind people are without an understanding that their own souls thirst for spiritual growth.

Outside of divine order, the joy of individuality is unknown. Most people have been unaware that their living souls extend into the Heavens and are one with the Lord of creation. Being willing to receive knowledge opens the heart to the revelation of wisdom, which in turn leads to life's eternal purpose. Oneness is revealed within the soul as life responds and receives everlasting Love.

"Why was I on earth?

Living with a free will subjected to resistance, my spiritual aptitude developed; I became a brighter, more lively being. I conceived a passion to spiritually evolve in Heaven's intelligence by entering earth's time line. I wanted to gather together with God's most ambitious friends. Given physical time, I will develop willpower in my faith by living courageously, helping my spiritual evolution.

By receiving an eternal soul, my gift of life, I chose to fulfill my Creator's purpose in my intelligent design.

When souls become mortal, as in infancy, their previous choices are forgotten. The passion to love the Creator is under the veil of humanity; the value of self-actualization begins to emerge out of uncertainty about the Holy Spirit. Through free choice, true Love is secured. When in perfect oneness with Heaven, the fullness of understanding of life is unveiled.

"I will grow in the Garden of Life to befriend the Love that created me."

Who Am I

When is my time to answer by rhyme
These ancient questions of the brave
Where amid this gift of life I lift my voice
To join the saints from their graves
How does one mere man sift through the sand
To find his heart and what it craves
Who am I to question the highest deity
How the meek of the earth will save
What souls will rise with words of praise
As I admit that by one man's wit
Set on fire an eternal blaze
In the spirit, I can hear it
Within this reality is
Pure divine order in my days

17

The Center of Creation

When God asked for a resting place, we were being invited to take part in a covenant, a Love agreement. God's desire is to further establish Heavenly friends within his creation. God calls to humanity to cooperate in providing a dwelling place and to continue blooming in the fruit of the spirit, going forward in Love's spiritual evolution through creation. We are being prepared to share in Heaven's creative orchestration by giving our best while bringing out the best in others.

On a mountain, away from the lovely melody that flowed through Paradise, I sat on the ground, holding my knees. About thirty feet behind us were two mighty angels standing quietly in the trees. The air was fresh and I looked up to see the top of the throne.

I saw an enormous celestial tree, and at the top, a huge gorgeous fountain continually creating a streaming waterfall of living light. Around the outskirts were many clouds filled with sleeping saints. Far in the distance above the Most High were shapes of swirling, glowing, wonderful golden worlds. Although I did not witness the full magnitude of our majestic God, I observed an aura of great wisdom permeating from above and beyond the crown of the celestial tree.

God's breath is pure Love pouring through creation in an orchestration of a new Heaven by and through our collective consciousness, creating a new earth.

Looking down, I could see an abyss of darkness as I watched multitudes of busy angels bringing prayers to the foot of the throne. *"Thus says the Lord: 'Heaven is my throne, and the earth is my footstool; what is the house that you would build for me, and what is the place of my rest?'"* (Isaiah 66:1). As we sat on a cliff, we witnessed the perfect regime of Heaven's Lovely administration.

Resting on the mountainside, basking in the breezes of God's breath, I was able to rationally think in pure clarity through my extension of God, my Holy Spirit. The Tree of Life is the most magnificent, fruitful, emanating light, multiplying God's glorious family. God's will and purpose is increasing Heaven's elaborate family through building multidimensional relationships.

On the outskirts of Paradise, sitting on a mountain looking up at Heaven's celestial Tree of Life, I felt calm, cool, and collected. An eminent domain of God's consciousness extends in elegance and reigns throughout the firmament, orchestrating the expansion of this universe. Loving, surging, white (fire); marvelous, vibrant, living, and colorful faith from earth's hearts was continually flowing up the center and raining throughout.

As we sat in the fresh mist of God's breath, I felt very centered in the reality of our Creator's Loving fountain of life known to us as the throne of God.

The foundation below Paradise appeared to be very clean and dark. As living water or liquid light streams from the throne, angels moving in the current of Love carry in the prayers and good intentions from earth to the foot of the throne. As they alight on the foot of the Tree of Life or the throne, there is a blast of the White Light of God's wisdom. Faster than the speed of light, angels come and go, producing a display of brilliantly intelligent lights booming with faith at the footstool of God.

Flowing up through the center of the Tree of Life, in an alignment with the laws of creation, in the structure of the divine will of our Lord, faithful prayers receive their response in pure wisdom. Where faith is alive a connection is made. Angels, were messengers of new ideas and insights. They buried seeds of light in the secret

The Center of Creation

chambers of earth's hearts.

Faith filled prayers intervene with the heart of God with humble, sweet intentions creating volumes of pure new life abounding throughout Heaven and earth. The Tree of Life inhales human energy fields; the wishes and concerns lifted up in faith and exhaled produce Loving, pure, clean White Light in spiritual wisdom. In faithful assurance, we experience our consciousness in the Holy Spirit aligning with Heaven.

There were additional bands of angels flowing throughout Heaven's neighborhoods, rolling in waves of life. The angels moved in response to the faith of believers' Love, creating sweet music in rhythm; all increased the course of Heaven's flow. Every enlightened mention, intention, and prayer penetrated the heart of our compassionate Lord. "There is a river whose streams make glad the city of God, the holy habitation of the Most High" (Psalms 46:4).

The breath of our Lord is continually responding, sending new surges of the White Light into the river of life that extends throughout our living universe. When a person first discovers his or her extended soul, he or she becomes one in unity with his or her spiritual family. Then everyone rejoices. There are great celebrations, flowers bloom, and the awakening of every soul's self-discovery creates a whirlwind of joy from the breath of God throughout Heaven.

The water-supported life flows in lovely music all the way into each believer's Heavenly neighborhood. Arising out of the preeminent excellence of God's mouth, formations swirl into the air—flowing music that gave spiritual life to creation. The people on earth are blessed. Immanuel, being God with us, is blessed, and Heaven rejoices. "You guide me with your counsel and afterwards you will receive me to glory" (Psalms 73:24).

Our families and friends in Heaven are continually in connection with us. We are intimately reasoning together, guided by Love through our lives' Holy Spirit. In this process of intercessory prayer, we are spiritually evolving. As we learn to listen to our little premonitions, our intuition strengthens to give us guidance along our life's way.

Heaven is orchestrated and thus fully organized, with saints overseeing it's lineages. Regardless of our doctrine or culture, each soul who endeavors to receive Love's light of truth connects with new life in their Holy Spirit.

Resting there in the fragrance of God's intelligence, I watched angels illuminating in colorful arrays. They moved faster than lightening, bringing prayers to the bottom of the Tree of Life.

Intertwined within the universe in pure consciousness, I was reminded of my endearing generosity. I felt like the lady who poured her precious perfume on the feet of Jesus. Earlier, we had danced in the music in Paradise. We experienced the outer courts as we witnessed creation implementing God's desires through archangels and their hierarchies. We viewed the center of all the consciousnesses arranging music that orchestrated Heaven. Our soul's intimate Love connection is in the kingdom of God.

River of Life

Beyond my cosmic vision of land, sky, and sea
Immenseness upholds much greater than me
How do I know this? How can it be?
Some say it is grace that allows me to see
In the paths of the deep of the universal sea
We all travel out of space-time, into eternity
Bonded by love, our light shines consciously
Carried through the river of life into infinity
Our light is in rhythm, intrinsically ready
Orchestrated by God's gentle integrity
Life lights my reality, omnipotence through me

18

Looking Past Earth's Chaos

I celebrated living music and color with the grace of Heaven's choir. Beneath the center of creation, below the rushing flow of radiant angels, beyond the dimension of Paradise, I saw another planet. Far below, hanging in our galaxy, the sky was indigo blue. The planet appeared to have black storm clouds moving all over it. As I looked closer, I began to feel very uneasy and remote.

I asked myself, "What is it?"

My spirit said, "You are looking at Earth."

I was stunned and became earnest.

I asked, "Is this the same Earth that I left?"

Looking down at the result of humanity's obstruction, I saw clouds filled with toxic, fuming gases that had formed from greed, lust, and rage, which led to the creation of blind, brute beasts. The thick, dark clusters of destructive energy fields had the semblance of a stealthy presence as it swarmed over the planet. I saw smoky, dark, colors moving around Earth. I looked closer to see that these were not dark shadows at all but rather live, snakelike creatures with open mouths; they were like a threatening tornado. *"He bowed the Heavens and came down; thick darkness was under his feet"* (Psalms

18:9).

The dark, collective consciousness swirled high above Earth in the form of swarming reptiles. The color black indicated separation, which causes emptiness and personifies creatures that live for consumption, dividing, and sequestering. Life-sucking energies roamed in the air above Earth, causing spiritual pressures and harm to humanity, especially to those who deny the authority in the living Love of God.

Underneath the life-sucking terrestrial devils, I saw glimmers of stunning, crystallized Lights—spiritual reasoning resonating life. I saw splendid, sparkling diamonds—open hearts receiving living water—the fresh air of Heaven's consciousness—from angels. The beastlike creatures were not thirsty nor seeking lifeless souls without God's brilliant, Holy Spirit. Rather, vipers roamed around searching for people with the enthusiasm of pure consciousness who were unprotected. On the other hand, hearts who cherish everlasting life were protected in the light of God.

Now, in the light of God's grace, peace in divine order rules our hearts (2 Corinthians 3:14-16). Our great intercessor, Jesus, is the White Light of Love bringing the consolation of God, giving us an anchor in the river of life (Hebrews 6:16-20).

After Immanuel overcame the fear of death, he ripped from top to bottom the veil, removing humanity's spiritual blindness (Matthew 27:51).

Liberated in the spirit, our consciousness is unveiled so we can enter with boldness into our own sanctuary, our upper room within our higher, omnipotent Holy Self. We transcend into our higher dimension in the colorful clarity of Love in our Father's grace. A new and living way (Hebrews 10:18-22) takes rise in our hearts through our Holy Spirit for the dawning of our new day.

I remembered the counsel of my heart when I learned why there is so much suffering on earth. I recalled turning into the Light after being confronted by the dark entities on my way to Heaven. These dark, evil forces embody humans and animals because they are hungry. They survive by sustaining enough living humanity and living intelligence for their own consumption.

I saw that suffering and confusion congregated on earth, and dark smoke hovered in some cities where the people were under bondage, driven by anxiety and fear. In other places, through the mist of fear and degradation, there arose sweet prayers reaching for life.

When Jesus ripped the veil away, earth quaked, closing the chasm both in this dimension and in higher realms, making way for our angels to descend, revealing to us the light of truth (Matthew 27:51; Matthew 28:24).

Regardless of the religion, nationality, or the pathetic moral condition of each seeking heart, angels respond to everyone. Affluent angels carry their friends' and neighbors' prayers, the intervention from Heaven, radiating Love, opening up and creating paths to their connections with their families.

At this point, I was deciding how I could be happy on Earth in the light of Heaven. I had a deep bond with my children and I had been given this responsibility. I reasoned within my higher self-realizing that I needed to spiritually evolve.

I could see that some lost and disconnected souls were unable to connect with the light unless, some enlightened soul with caring intentions would turn on the light for them.

As I looked at earth, I realized that this was a juncture, a place to make another life-changing decision. The whole time I was in Heaven, not one reflection of earth's woes had entered my mind, except in view of our spiritual evolution.

Now, I was confronted with the law of my soul; my Love covenant and my eternal soul is one with my Creator's purpose for giving me life. I quickly acknowledged by spiritual discernment and had clarity of my soul's interconnection with God. I remembered my Love commitment and desire to be born into a circumstance that would allow me to develop a passion to reach for true wisdom and find peace in the light of supplication.

Aware that the answers to life's inquiries are in the secrets of creation and are continually rejuvenating within me one instant at a time, I trusted in a new way. I honored God who invested valuable life within me.

I looked to my right, and there I saw two babies, a boy and a girl, around the age of four. They were both very precious to my heart as they sat waiting for me. The boy had a bouncing giggle and eyes that twinkled as he smiled at me. The baby girl sat holding onto her big toe; she was patiently waiting for me to pick her up. I found a new, deep Love in our connection.

I didn't rationalize that they were mine, but rather that I was their provider. I glanced around but found no one else to care for them. I considered that I had been put on the spot and needed to make a decision without interrupting the flow of Heaven's harmony.

I weighed my options as I stood on the threshold of life and death, pondering the void of weightlessness. In viewing the planet entangled with black reptiles, I was fully aware that this decision was much like the one to be born in the first place. In pure Love, I could see that by entering earth's time line, my decision and my consciousness would have a ripple effect and influence everyone in my Garden of Life in Heaven.

I recalled the courageous intercessions that had passed me by in the root of the Tree of Life. My soul had been converted as I was baptized in Heaven's living water, reborn in the White Light into Heaven's immaculate conception. I had been born again into one with Heaven, transformed into perfect unity. In a blessed peace and perfect Love, I had shared heart-to-heart interactions with my closest loved ones and had come in touch with God's giant friends.

The prospect to reemerge on earth with more challenges would accelerate my spiritual development and increase my velocity in my celestial arrangement. My spiritual teacher and comforter, my extension, my Holy Spirit, gently teaches my fragile heart.

I remembered my life review before I was born into earth's time line. I have a new certainty that every moment, I earn a deeper trust in my Creator Lord.

I came to grips with my covenant agreement that by my living a challenging life, this would set me up to be more receptive to the wisdom of God. My life on earth seemed to be shortened from Heaven's vantage point. In order for my Love to increase, my effectiveness to improve, and to understand the pure virtue of divine reasoning, the kind that orchestrates creation, I will embrace Love by my free choice and align my consciousness with the Creator.

In the far distance, earth was unfamiliar and cold. En route to

Heaven, after I veered away, I overcame fear's grip and in disdain, I transcended the foul, stealthy, interdimensional interferences when I focused on the authenticity of God. I found the boldness of my belief, the breath of God within. I discovered that in darkness, we reach for the light and therein is our source of understanding. Heaven's consciousness is the organized structure in the Holy Spirit, the mind of our Lord.

I recalled that in my life review, Heaven's White Light reflects a colorful, intelligent radiance that breaks the bands of darkness. My light so shined, and I entered into an assurance, a confidence that I needed for the rest of my life. I glanced at my omnipotent silver cloud then at my boy and girl twins, and my heart filled with compassion to help me make the right decision. Without good-byes or second-guessing, I dived down into earth's galaxy.

In the spirit, I live in a higher domain, designed for a specific inheritance and am preordained to progress to fulfill God's precise intensions. I am progressing in spiritual evolution for all our destinies. As a snowflake grows in symmetry when it falls to the ground, I am growing into the likeness of my original spiritual design. I shall be refined into Heaven's real estate, meant for an explicit location and purpose. Heaven was my beginning and is my eternal home.

(I wrote this at age ten)

The Worldly Phase

Here I stand upon a star
looking at a world of sin
Thinking deeply why we are
and wondering who I am
What is the answer
to an open heart
Who leads us on our way
Does our conscience do its part
Or do we follow the worldly phase
Is Love the answer to our emptiness
Or does fear seem to guide
Would God above
please and fulfill us
Or would this hurt our foolish pride

19

Entering Earth's Galaxy from Paradise

God's eyes of Love are watching us spiritually grow. When I approached the cosmic order of earth's galaxy, I felt out of synch; a shift was occurring in my conscience. My sense of wholeness began to fade. I pondered about where I was headed, although I could not remember clearly. From a high mountain outside of the throne, I headed toward the thick darkness.

A feeling of emptiness along with memories of Heaven echoed through my mind. All my soul remembered was that life holds much more meaning. I felt far removed from pure divine reasoning. In Heaven, I had had vivid clarity in one continual flow of coherent light. I lost my sense of direction as I felt earth's collective consciousness assume my essence.

I floated outside a lighted room with dimly lit, plate-glass windows. In one room, a nurse looked right at me but didn't see my spiritual aura. She was glancing through the plate-glass window as she worked on a report. Thoroughly disconnected from my cold, pale, physical body, it looked peculiar to me. I pondered what I should do, knowing that my options were limited.

After a loud thud, the most terrible certainty of being dead weight bolted into my body. Every slight movement in my aching body had dire consequences. Moments before I entered my body, all my senses had moved as one. As soon as I reentered my body, my thought process remained centered so that all pain was intensely amplified. My five physical senses interfered with and fueled the confusion that cluttered my mind. I began questioning my Holy Spirit. The horrible weight of gravity reminded me of my inability to help myself.

My brain was bombarded with environmental influences.

I tried to pick up where I had left off. I remembered the desensitizing energy fields full of the collective consciousness of obscure, irrational reasoning. It seemed that I needed to compartmentalize my thought processes to find rational thought. I was incoherent to the divine order in my spiritual mind. I entered into a time line in which I repeatedly encountered many unsettling questions. I had an empty feeling as though I should be somewhere else. *"But the Comforter, which is the Holy Ghost (Spirit), the Father will send in my name, he will teach you all things and bring to your remembrance whatsoever I have said to you"* (John 14:26).

I opened my eyes as medical technicians wheeled me into surgery. I remember riding in a blue, industrial-type elevator that opened on both sides. As we edged out into the hospital hall, a nurse ran alongside the bed.

Leaning over me, watching my eyes, she kept screaming, "Surgery!"

As I awakened to my body riddled with pain, I had a vague memory of what was going on in earth's time line before I departed. For the previous fifteen days before I gave birth—before my tour of Heaven—I had been fed intravenously. I didn't have enough room for two babies, two placentas, and a functional stomach.

I shared one room with five girls. One by one they came, gave birth, and after three days, went home. Every one of us was classified as high risk. Diabetes, overweight, too young, too old, and one with epilepsy—all deliveries had gone smoothly until mine. I was too small to carry twins. My daughter could not respond to my contractions because she was wedged underneath my ribs.

Consequently, I had undergone a C-section, episiotomy, and

additional internal alterations. My psychological and spiritual alterations caused a much greater consequence. Along with a complete blood transfusion, I was adjusting to an increased spiritual sensitivity and physical trauma while learning to listen to my Holy Spirit. My whole physical body was still in shock and very bruised.

After surgery, I had stitches inside and out. My chest was burned and I was swollen, black-and-blue from my neck to my legs. I spent an additional two weeks in the hospital, making my stay there over a month.

My bed was surrounded with fragrances from fresh flowers. I appreciated them, though they were drab compared to Heaven's intelligently engaging flowers that danced and smiled in delight. Love from Heaven's consciousness comes with insightful remedies on how to enjoy the present.

A nurse came around the corner with both babies, one in each arm. My specialist, Dr. Haswell, followed her in and told me I was the proud mother of "a healthy little miracle girl and a healthy baby boy." He was calm, sincere, and thankful for my life. My doctor was a devout Catholic, a man known for his healing hands. I believe it was his prayer and his angel that took me to his church, the large downtown Catholic cathedral. He has since passed on to be with his Heavenly family.

He gently assured me that everyone was pleasantly surprised that my baby girl was healthy. He shared that the medical team all rejoiced when they saw my vital signs return.

He told me, "You are blessed to be here and have a healthy little girl. We thought that she was without oxygen for too long."

I didn't understand the liability that he and the hospital could have risked due to my second dose of anesthesia. He stood at the foot of my bed, apologizing for my unfortunate experience, telling me, "We were all praying. We thought we lost you. We are so relieved."

For a while, Dr. Haswell and I peacefully shared a private, meaningful conversation as he explained that I had additional stitches inside me due to the abrupt removal of the second fetus. (My medical record indicates that they removed my baby girl without making an incision. In other words, they ripped me open.)

He smiled and said, "But we saved her life. We had a close call. I was concerned that we would lose both of you. But you may never be able to carry another baby."

I was thirty-two and had twins; all was well with me. What seemed to be a grievous misfortune was actually spiritually transforming. With the help of Heaven's consciousness, we furthered the integration and advancement of our whole celestial family.

Right before they left, I asked, "Why did you stand by the window for such a long time after I flat-lined?"

His eyes lit up. He smiled and asked, "You saw me praying for you?" He was pleased I had mentioned it.

I answered, "Yes, your prayers were with me."

We had a nice conversation for a while, and before he left, he said, "You see, the law requires us to save the baby before the mother. I prayed about that. I wanted to save you, too."

They put me in a unit called Recovery. For the additional two weeks that I spent in Recovery, I sensed the infirmity of those in the rooms around me. Some were dying with fatal diseases. When the nurses talked to patients, and the patients responded, I felt their pain come through their voices. Sometimes, I could tell what kind of ailment they were trying to suppress with painkillers.

With an acute reaction to sounds and lights, my world had changed. I acknowledged an enhanced ability to see what people were thinking.

During the night, I was awakened by flashbacks. I was devastated by the contrast of Heaven and earth. In Heaven, everything is alive and in harmony. This made earth seem like a huge, pointless struggle.

At that time, I had a lot to assimilate and bring into fundamental reasoning. I wanted to share about Heaven to alleviate my own physical feelings; I felt generously excited, yet Heaven didn't seem relevant to anyone in my immediate surroundings. I received a refreshing confidence that my life had significant value in a more important place.

As I came into sufficient consciousness, I was in two worlds. Every one of my family and friends seemed odd. Some old friends were strangers to me. My mother and sister said that my voice sounded better and my demeanor had improved. We all had some adjusting to do. Most of the time, I tried to find the right words to mention something about Heaven, but the concepts would not come because I couldn't seem to make a connection in the spiritual realm.

I loved people who lived in the present tense. We flowed together even when we were perfect strangers. I found myself answering questions before they were asked.

One night, much later, after I returned home, when the twins were asleep, I was talking with my husband as we sat in the back yard. The sky was dark. As we looked into the sky, I felt my connection with Heaven's consciousness and I wanted to share it.

I must have shouted at him, "We came from Heaven!" He was amazed how I spoke with such deep conviction when I said, "We occupy a specific location in the sky. In spirit we will return home!"

He jumped to his feet and loudly answered by repeating, "I believe it!"

Heaven's Love reaches past a person's intellect and nestles in the heart. The fire of Love finds the deepest crevices in the core of the soul's self-identity, an inner knowing or intelligence. By honoring our Creator with a thankful attitude for life, we enter into our own creativity. This is our way to grow in grace. This shapes our individuality. Being grateful brings out the best in ourselves and one another. Being willing to try brings alive our faith. We resonate joy through our morphing fields, ultimately transcending our humanity's limitations. The Lord unfolds our souls and we build our destinies.

This life on earth is our opportunity to willingly excel in our Creator's multidimensional environment that the New Testament refers to as the kingdom of God. Each soul's eternal life is continually excelling through dimensions, developing new ways to create spiritual habits. Our Holy Spirit is the light of pure consciousness. Unlike a plant, our consciousness is gifted with a free will so that by becoming spiritually intelligent we grow in God's light of grace.

In becoming accountable to our Creator in our ongoing relationship, our soul receives new courage daily, and we see how things are first being orchestrated in spiritual timing. In this turn of the ages, our souls are evolving new life by our Love, through our willingness and cooperation, and from our personal interconnections with Heaven, which keeps us in the flow.

Religion without a relationship with the Holy Spirit is reliant on the established doctrines, each with limitations made by the collective consciousness of that belief system. Religion, without a willingness to trust in the presence of our Holy Spirit, changes consciousness and defines accountability as being in good standing with that particular religious denomination. Religions that teach that to be okay with God you must first keep the ordinances of the church are taking away personal accountability.

We are here to become personally accountable to the Creator, the author of our eternal soul. We create spiritual willpower by overcoming passivity. Through our willingness to understand our eternal purpose, we find a new realm of faith that changes or shifts our attitudes. Our individual consciousness receives the Love of God and attunes to our Holy Spirit. We live in an environment interconnected with the intelligences of our Heavenly families. Our creativity excels from boredom and lifelessness. We accept that new insights arise from our good choices, and this is great encouragement.

In the awakening of our faith, we discover our individuality. By shifting into a more expanded awareness, our spiritual life begins to understand pure Love. Heaven's consciousness comes with insightful remedies on how to enjoy the present. This is the process of self-discovery as we become more accountable and attentive to our timeless oneness with our Creator.

Entering Earth's Galaxy from Paradise

Boldness Breathes Light

Dare to care enough to face the darkness
To tangle, and still to my Lord be true
Earth's imposters hide behind logistics
To distort and challenge a good man's view
A book written by ancient Romans to subdue and fake
Mixed pure truth with theory, to impose upon the weak
To bring conflict into religion for perpetual critique
In the light of archangels, we see the enemy break
God's grace resonates from Heaven's glories
Angels hold back the destruction of evil treaties
Evolved in Heaven's consciousness, we stand at ease
Strength in brilliance shine through Michael's armies
In faith, we take position and in spiritual prestige
My preference is silenced, my boldness breathes
God's presence comes through bright orbs of peace
With our own hierarchies, we are in besiege
Heaven's light prevails as the contender grieves

PART II

Life after Death

Stephanie Grace and Jonathan Jason

20

Spiritual Awareness

I went to extremes to understand how to live happily. I found pleasure in the wonder of creation. Every year, the seasons brought change that caused all of the little creatures to readjust. In the spring, water transformed mountains, causing flowing rivers of flourishing life to cover winter's dead ground. In this busy world, I looked into the mysteries—the laws of creation—and I found God.

Like a child, I was amused with nature's timing, changing the face of earth without notice. Oysters are building valuable pearls, and silkworms are spinning silk without any comprehension of what they are doing. Humanity finds perfection in the gold and diamonds formed deep in the ground. Creation's life springs out of the dirt. New life is in response to light and water that come from the air.

Spiritual life is in the atoms that are hiding within all these life forms, and everyone's atoms are specifically designed to generate differently. I learned in science class that atoms act in much the same way as our universe. While seeds, birds, and fish all develop distinctive features, I pondered and asked myself why. This brought me to the notion that all living creatures may have individual vantage points, all born in an arrangement with a grand design.

Amid my musing at the mysteries in nature, I could see many hidden messages were to be found only in our spiritual relationship with the Lord of creation. When I was honest with myself, I had no preconceived opinions or prejudices.

Little by little, I accepted that over time I would understand why some people are very happy and others aren't. When I was little, I prayed, "If there is a Heaven or a God, just give me a glimpse enough to know, and I will be happy."

When I was in my early twenties, the first big commitment I made was working as a full-time missionary. Here, I thought, I could enjoy learning about creation's mysteries while helping orphans and the homeless.

For five years in Oklahoma, Arkansas, and Colorado, God answered my prayer; I did the tough jobs. I served while I learned to think rationally. I got up in the quiet morning when everything was still and dark. I began to examine my mind for spiritual insights not really aware that I was searching to know my own Holy Spirit's Love. Soon, I had the understanding that to listen well I needed to shut up and sit up. I discovered how to listen to my soul for timeless truths that are anchored in the laws of creation.

Many times, it took me more than an hour in silence before I could be receptive to my soul's Holy Spirit. Although I felt refreshed in the stillness of my morning time, I wasn't sure how to truly like myself. After listening well, with my mind cleared of useless chatter, I began to understand how to enjoy my learning process. Listening to my positive premonitions changed my perceptions of who God is.

God's happiness is deeply ingrained in my inner knowing of oneness with creation. Seeing the divine order yet elaborate way God works through creation improved my whole attitude. As time went on, I liked myself more and more as I learned to be receptive to my heart. I sensed what I believed was God Loving me.

Our self-perceptions are discovered in our integration of the spiritual senses of one another. While each person has a different vantage point—each with his or her own reflection on truth to live by—our hearts bring together the flow in perfect rhythm, causing us to be mindful that we are an expression of God's joy.

Just like a flower blooming, in spending time alone and in contemplation, I found my heart being bathed in my Holy Spirit. God's pure breath is the living water, giving me a gentle peace. I am not more astute or religious, but rather I am able to recognize my mind's interpretation of my intuition coming with new spiritual insights dawning in my heart and soul. My heart received understanding from my greater source; my higher intelligence caused new feelings to come alive. Although I didn't know how to maintain peace, caused me to began to trust my intuition.

I became aware of a more amiable sense of goodness that spiritually blended with everyone around me. I looked for people I could relate to. In missionary work, I noticed an array of belief systems coming from many denominations, associations, and cultures.

Volunteers who dedicate their lives to a greater cause have deep convictions about what they believe is truth. Each one holds to their beliefs as if his or her life depends on it. Some missionaries were exceptionally happy to make a connection with me. Their religious affiliations seemed insignificant to me. Everyone who knows how to trust in the Most High authority shared a spiritual Love and freedom with other believers.

The happy missionaries whose genuine joy came from their souls caused me to be in tune with my higher self. "You shall know the truth and the truth shall set you free" (John 8:32). We shared new insights about how to solve the orphans' problems. Our relationship was not based on our culture or our perceptions about religion, but rather we held to a subliminal inner knowing of a guiding presence of goodness. We understood a spiritual mystery we call Love, God, or perhaps Our Helper.

Sometimes in our evening gatherings, we would refer to the Holy Spirit as a presence. We discussed how to help certain troubled orphans. When we quieted our minds, we all received similar messages that contained solutions that we hadn't otherwise thought of. With this new wisdom came a sweet peace, and more all the time.

One of my tasks included preparing breakfast for about thirty people. Missionaries from Guinea, Nicaragua, Jamaica, Haiti, and other third-world countries would come in to rest, share their testimony, and get revived enough to return to their work. Morning after morning during breakfast, I heard some of the missionaries express their discontentment. It was heart wrenching for me to feel the grief from those who did not realize how blessed they were because of their many sacrifices.

I noticed two kinds of love: People share a love for earthly sensations that is found by focusing on temporary emotional feelings. Understanding divine Love is to know God's multidimensional Love. The kind of love that is most effective comes through our Creator's pure justice that prevails within and reigns through our rational thought, uplifting to all of our consciousnesses.

This was my reality check. Both human love and God's Love enhance the emotions of the giver in a similar manner, creating generous motivation and a sense of euphoria.

Some missionaries trusted a higher authority. All who maintained happiness trusted Love would come with insight and direction and in good timing. We had an inner knowing that true Love resonated from one another's presence. I could easily see the difference in the volunteers who became missionaries because they were moved by compassion for third-world orphans. Divine Love that comes from above stabilizes and strengthens in an ongoing relationship. The ones who loved with God's Love shared a blissful sense of humor that they received by trusting God's greater purpose for each individual need.

A good number of happy missionaries found life very fulfilling. These were the missionaries who lived in peace and reported what they referred to as miracles. I felt calm and collected when I was around them, the same peace that I found in my long walks in the country while pondering spiritual life.

I associated their love and freedom with little creatures in nature. I noticed that creation is smooth and steady, always in perfect continuity, causing pure life to spring out of nowhere—sort of like the smiles of the happy missionaries.

Some children had been orphaned from loving, nurturing parents, although most came in without any family bond. During the five years that we lived together, trusting in the Creator, I worked for a year with thirty juvenile delinquents who came from overcrowded detention centers. All were from broken homes, had broken laws, and were very bewildered. At that age, they were in the process of self-discovery—to learn what they believed and to find their self-identity.

All of the juveniles came from dysfunctional families. Most of their parents' priorities were caught up in their professions, social agendas, or religious work. Some were abused and others were neglected. Most of these children were taught the traditional teachings, including to honor your father and mother—even those parents who brought deception and evil into their homes.

In Exodus 20:12, "honor" meant to have the "heavy" realization that God provided your long life through your parents. In Matthew 15: 4-6, when Jesus was talking about the traditions of man, he used this same commandment. "Honor," as Jesus used it, meant to "value" the gift of God more than your parents. Matthew 10:34-37 and Luke 12:53: "Jesus said, 'I came not to send peace but division… that a man's foes shall be that of his own household. *He that loves his father or mother more than me is not worthy of me.*'"

In Matthew 15:10-14, Jesus spoke in parables, calling the teachers of traditions and the commandments of men defiled by their words and blind leaders of the blind.

Knowing that human love provides a comfort zone as does traditional religious teachings, in order to rise above human limitations, God's Love would need to intervene. Certain abused children could then accept their freedom from bad family ties only by becoming aware of this greater Love. This situation provided me with incentive to create a stronger will to find my light of divine Love in the midst of the prevailing discontentment of missionaries, orphans, and juveniles.

I wanted to help them find their own self-respect. Before I could point a lost orphan toward his or her own personal value and through rational thought, I first would need to understand how to provide an uplifting, loving, influential environment. I decided that

God gave me a mind to sort out what hindered them in their search.

I wanted to be a good missionary, so I got up early and observed the morning dawn as my consciousness became more alive, much in the same way as the sun changes the face of the earth.

I took my liberty to heart, believing I could find an all-inclusive way to respond to life's challenges. Being young and optimistic, I believed the Scriptures literally, especially the ones about fasting (Matthew 4:2).

Fasting took a great deal of discipline. I went on long expeditions in the country because I loved to be reminded of the vast transformations in nature. I made it through a ten-day fast only drinking juice. My spiritual attentiveness increased so much that I went on a thirty-day fast only drinking water. Then, I made myself drink only vegetable juice.

I learned to disregard distractions so that I could center in on my spiritual reasoning. As my five senses were less active, my rational thought was clearly in tune with my spirit.

My prayer life was enhanced. My spiritual and emotional senses responded more observantly. I looked into the Scriptures to find understanding where divine Love arises over emotionally disabling family ties. When some children received the clarity of God's Love, they no longer felt intimidated by the traditional teachings that had kept them in their confusing family relationships.

I realized that the spirit of God first moves in spiritual order. "By the washing of regeneration and renewing of the Holy Spirit… we might become heirs (in the river) of eternal life" (Titus 3:5-7).

Gradually, some children found their real joy in their life's process of self-discovery. By sharing their new-felt freedoms, through their work and play, their involvement caused an inner knowing of their own personal value. More and more, in sharing their gifts and talents, their courage began to grow.

My Loving premonitions were my spiritual senses causing me to be mindful that, together, we were making great progress. It wasn't up to me to be a fixer or a healer but rather to be spiritually fascinated with God's perfect timing, rearranging circumstances that kept us in peace.

Our courage was contagious, bringing us together—soul and spirit—into one Love. My reward for seeking the truth was in my own self-discovery. My subliminal yet courageous contributions came through my presence, blending with others as we were being uplifted and helping stabilize true happiness in ourselves and the children.

In some mysterious way, I, too felt that I was piercing through my psychological behaviors as I overcame the walls of my cocoon or the fear of what spiritually blind people might think. The more we lived by faith and trusted for the divine intervention of Love, the more we found new spiritual freedoms, just as butterflies flying in community toward their destinies.

Divine Love

Beyond our earthly possibilities is Heaven's prosperities.
Our soul's Love signature sends grace filled frequencies.
Our divine intuition unveils our silent wish and mission.
 Ringing from our hearts echoes colors of our prisms.
  As the author of divine time is showing us the way,
   In deep passion we are asking in sweet simplicity.
   Transcending human love we ask simultaneously.
    Together in adoration and wonder filled unity.
    We listen for a fresh new Love to give liberally.
   God's Love flows beautifully in divine generosity,
  Our new day is dawning for the whole world to see,
 Through all who truly care love extraordinaire is reality.
The bright and morning star arises in pure sweet honesty.
Today in Heaven's starlight, we understand subliminally
  In this Love my Lord I hear. You too are asking me;
    "Today my dear, what do you want of me?"

21

Mission on Earth from Paradise

Our Lord's dispensation of light is reigning, divine Love and through our consciousness orchestrates our living universe. Before my spiritual journey through the White Light to the center of creation, I really only had a vague notion of my true, divine Love. My eyes were opened to an understanding to a living Love that penetrates the depth of my soul with comforting clarity.

The laws of creation came from Heaven and are governed by God's pure Love here to build loving relationships. Through our experience on earth, we are creating our spiritual essence. By listening well to our conscience, we overcome temptations while developing our unique souls, which are our Heavenly personalities.

In nature, we observe how God's creatures lovingly nurture their young. This helps us to better understand Love. God's true purpose for entrusting us and giving us a measure of faith that first works by human love is to give us opportunity to grow in grace-filled friendships.

At first, human love is shown in generosity although not necessarily reflecting spiritual edification to our eternal soul. Humanity's spiritual consciousness may be only open to the five physical senses and initially unable to realize divine Love. Without knowing the Love of God, all humanity has is a love that is influenced by the five physical senses, which stems from environmental influences causing emotional thoughts.

I learned that unconditional love can come from human energy fields and then grows into divine Love. In our Creator's intelligent design, human love is elementary to show us that through the laws of nature, we evolve into the fullness of our true Love in unity and oneness.

Our personal value is first known through human love. Human love is given to reinforce our human connections, a sentiment of appreciation and good intentions. Through loyalty and kindness, it secures our human emotional stability. This nurturing kind of love is first a natural reaction in the physical body that can eventually understand and develop to flow in spiritual Love.

When we accept that we are embodying an eternal soul, God keeps our full attention by revealing pure Love coming through our own consciousness. A mystery of life is in the unfolding of beautiful flower buds. In a similar way, we open our hearts in the realization of our gracious, Loving God. Loving light brings to life our spiritual senses, enabling courageous insight to rise out of human love. This life is given us to fulfill this higher cause. Time is our gift to understand Love in a new light.

Divine Love works by faith to strengthen patience when human emotions fail. Our pilot light of truth receives an inner prompting to Love, unfolding within as a water lily. Our peaceful grace grows into a sacred bond. Heaven opens our understanding as we listen to the subliminal unction of our intuition, and our spiritual senses come alive.

My courage comes in knowing that my life on earth means more in Heaven than here. God's greater purpose improved my attitude and my confidence to stand in faith. The Holy Spirit shines into our hearts in a new and living grace every day, giving us clarity of God's Love.

In this turn of the ages, spiritual oneness is being unveiled as humanity's purpose ascends into a new comprehensive interaction with Heaven. We experience new expressions flowing from our own soul, while our true Love is enabling other people to become mindful of their spiritual senses.

For years, I heard people use the name of Jesus like a loud weapon while telling God what his words meant. Jesus's name holds the energy fields in our collective consciousness; the knowledge of the authority of God's Love authority is integrated with the willpower of every true believer. (Jesus Christ is Immanuel who is God with us.) It isn't the actual emotion, loudness, or notion in speaking the name but rather an inner union known within our spiritual senses. Love is divine order and our reigning authority; our consciousness that stills the storm and calms the sea with three faithful words: *peace be still*.

It is written that Jesus marveled at the soldier as he said to his follower, "I have not found so great faith…go your way and as you have believed, for you, it is done" (Matthew 8:5). He describes "faith" as the understanding of Love's divine authority. This is a mention of ranks or hierarchies in the kingdom of Heaven.

Now, I see why Jesus asked, "Is it easier to say, be saved or be healed?" (Matthew 9:5). He was asking how a person would prefer to receive the light of Love from Heaven—through a realization found in a covenant relationship or through becoming physically healthy. Jesus's conscience gave humanity the ability to receive healing and to save its own soul from desolation.

An example of why Jesus told of the rich man and the poor man was to show how our universe works. Angels of Heaven carried the poor man to Abraham's side (to his bosom or consciousness). The rich man died and was buried in torment where he could see the light of Abraham's soul far off.

In human love, the rich man, even in anguish, desired to help his brothers. His human love was intellectually strong enough to argue for his brothers. Abraham's answer to the rich man was, "They have Moses and the prophets; let them hear them" (Luke 16:22).

Our Lord explained, "The light of truth is in the presence of the words of the prophets, their voices are resonating pure consciousness throughout our universe." The soldier understood God's living resonance of Love's authority. The rich man responded to the White Light of Father Abraham. Through divine Love, our Comforter is guiding us all to our destiny's providence.

Opportunity Accepted

Boldness is to believe that Justice will prevail
We honor what is good and determine to be real
Overcome one ego, all-else becomes so frail
We learn to listen well by choices that fail
Our divine Comforter teaches us to think
Like Immanuel, we learn from our mistake
Find balance to stretch our willpower to the brink
Blessed are the hopeful for they shall be
Ignited by the White Light in Heaven's harmony

22

God's Breath of Life

"*Firmament*" means expanding in its original biblical use. Our consciousness is expanding Heaven. *"Let there be a firmament in the midst of the waters, and let it divide the waters from the waters. God made the firmament and divided the waters, which were above the firmament... God called the firmament Heaven"* (Genesis 1:6-8).

God breathed the breath of life and man became a living, growing soul. God's breath is the White Light of Love, expanding life through our universe.

If Genesis is literal or symbolical, it was written in Hebrew a minimum of nine hundred to more than two thousand years before Christ was born (BC). Adam and Eve are the classic model for depicting human tendencies and weaknesses. The events in Genesis portray humanity choosing knowledge outside of God's will and timing. The result was "sin consciousness" and the stifling of their spiritual connection and disengaging their evolution.

Eden comes from a word that describes a royal city of pleasure. The Garden of Eden was a state of conscious pleasure. "Eve" in Hebrew means "to be alive as a human." "The Lord God made spring up every tree that is pleasant to the sight and good for food"

(Genesis 2:9). The Tree of Life was in the midst of the garden. Each living soul's gift of life has the "time to decide."

Human consciousness comes with the ability to make decisions. Decisions develop willpower that defines self-identity in relation to our self, one another, and to God. Our will is a gift of life given with time to empower us to make decisions.

The second tree is the Tree of Knowledge that gives understanding to the conscience or a moral aptitude. Spiritual knowledge revealed in the divine timing of God's will brings to life Heaven's consciousness.

When Eve was alone in the garden, she was offered personal power (a self-image) to be like a god: "You will (your will) become more influential..." Eve accepted the proposal of having power. Out of divine time, apart from the light of life, Eve chose to be on her own—to obtain personal power to usurp authority.

Adam, virtuous with pure consciousness, was seduced by his counterpart or by his own humanity. No longer in divine timing, unable to comprehend his loss, he found himself in a state of dread.

God said, "The day that you eat of the Tree of Knowledge, you shall surely die (become disconnected from your source)." Their (Eve's and Adam's) consciousnesses lost an ability to experience spiritual pleasure in the growth of their relationships. Sin consciousness preoccupied their minds, smothering them from sharing their spiritual Love.

Out of the divine timing of their spiritual growth, they lost their way. Without connection, they were blind to their purposes and incoherent to the beauty of their self-images made in the image of God.

Eve, a representative of humanity, seeks the road of least resistance. We humans, when we are separate from the light of life, many times are cowards in search of a quick fix. Adam and Eve were placed in Paradise and given an opportunity to develop willpower through becoming loyal to their Creator.

By free choice, human love adapts into a faithful response to divine Love. The kingdom of Heaven begins with God's multidimensional light of faith taking root in our soul. Our vibratory energy fields are transformed into the eternal life, expanding the kingdom of Heaven, growing Heaven's firmament.

We see many people around us living their entire lives suffering in blind bondage. Seeking to discover themselves outside of an understanding of their Heavenly connection, they are alone. This world's pretentious attitudes blind the heart to stay in a perpetual search for an easy way to be influential. A false sense of personal power sequesters the masses.

Our Holy Spirit is the extension of our individual soul and is our gift. The result of the lie in the garden of our life is to blind us so we will avoid God's terms and conditions and disregard our Heavenly connection.

If we get distracted, we disengage from our higher consciousness, and our ego can become entertaining. We should learn that vanity appeals to our ego. Our response to each unlikely situation should show us that we should get away from detrimental energy fields—where the collective consciousness of egotistical limitations rule—and that to live by faith, we need to see the frailty of our vanity. After we find ourselves drained, we learn how to discern and to shy away from ego-driven social agendas that result in emptiness and loss.

Those who are peacefully anchored in the river of living water have the power to make quality decisions. Along the way, the serpent, or knowledge of human limitation, offers earthly wisdom. Without the light of life, the power to persuade is limited to selfishness.

Charming ideas that appeal to our pride are no more than illusions to make us feel more influential. These lies infuse people with a haughty attitude as if knowledge, things, or connections with certain people or establishments could actually bring us true happiness.

In the biblical account of the Sumerian lady at the well, Jesus said, "If you knew the gift of God and who it is that is saying to you, 'Give me drink,' you would have asked him and he would have given you living water" (John 4:4–29).

Living water from Heaven nurtures the soul. The Tree of Knowledge is rooted and grounded in the living water that is flowing through our ancestral Tree of Life. This is in our garden where our saints, angels, and hierarchy dwell.

Our Heavenly families are continually available to nurture our growth. "All who will; come to the water of life and drink freely" (Revelation 22:17). God's light in my anatomy, or "atoms in me," is God's breath, the light of my life. Destiny's Next Answer (God's DNA) comes within our Love experience, changing our timing into divine timing, expanding our spiritual senses with infinity.

To love our neighbors as ourselves, our vantage points open, giving us spiritual insights that expand to extend our faith to work by Love. We choose to create lifestyles where we can receive courage to make our lives available to listen to our consciences. Our spiritual emotional endorphins, "our in-door friends," enlighten our souls so that in faith, we are attentive to our own truths.

The Holy Spirit surrounds us with angels influencing our Loving premonitions. Overall, our human personalities are shaped by ourselves. We enjoy responding through our free will, developing our own souls.

Our unique personalities eventually respond to our higher Love consciousnesses. We are then aware of our own interactions with our faith making our choices. When our own varieties of Love are our choices, we become aware of the expansion of our own self-made personalities. "We are the spice of life and the salt of the earth" (Matthew 5:13).

Jesus, being a direct descendant of God's DNA, cleaned the air with words that carried creative Love into our universe: "Already you are clean because of the word that I have spoken to you. Abide in me, and I in you. As the branch cannot bear fruit by itself, unless it abides in the vine, neither can you (grow), unless you abide in me" (John 15:4).

Heaven's Love is the multidimensional brilliance of God's consciousness expanding within our Love. This is spiritual life growing in the firmament –the living universe.

Jesus responded to a blind man and led him away from his observers and used his own spit (DNA) to touch his eyes. His spirit (atoms of light) penetrated the blind man's soul. Jesus asked him, "Do you see anything?" First, the blind man could only see in the spirit, "I see people, but they look like trees, walking." Then, Jesus laid his hands on him again; his physical vision became clear. Jesus then advised him, "Do not even enter the village." Saying, "Keep away from the people who do not understand because they will hurt your spiritual vision" (Mark 8:24-26).

Our spiritual attentiveness in divine Love is sacred and precious to our Lord. I make my early morning hours sacred; this is my time when I am in a deeper level of consciousness, searching for the deep waters, for more creative ways to open my consciousness to new realities. Spiritual awareness is a cognitive shift into a meditative state. When I center within my soul to listen to my Heavenly self in a quieter level, I go beyond my earthly self, and in trust, open my spiritual senses. I center within my own Holy Spirit and spread my invisible wings as I extend into pure consciousness.

My attention is drawn into my meditative state of mind that expands and organizes my reactions each time in a completely new way than when I am reacting to thoughts that come from my head. I accept the basis of my mind is willing to expand with the infinite.

As I center in God's presence, my thoughts come alive in greater understanding. I receive insight in creative "problem solving." Also, I discover ways to complete the little tasks in life. Whatever state I find my physical self in, I settle into my innermost being where Heaven opens my understanding. Here, I can see new insights of the character of God. This increases my soul's awareness of the actuality of the presence of an all-encompassing master of space who gave me free will to use time to grow in faith. My mind is renewed by my free choices. When I am in adoration, I am becoming one with my Creator as the light of my soul harmonizes with angels to prepare my circumstances.

Gabriel's radiantly, magnificently adorned angels follow Michael's colorful, powerful, gracefully adorned armies of guiding lights. I saw countless Heavenly groupings in symmetry, eloquent formations; celestial families in royally exquisite uniforms appearing to convey their Loving presence, waving at me in joyful victory.

Heaven continues to reveal to us the mighty God we serve to remind us that we are being ushered into the White Light of pure consciousness. Divine Love began in the creative breath of God. This same light is healing Love in the laws of creation that is revealed through relationships within every soul's trusting heart. *God's Holy*

Spirit is a widespread, expanding information network of lights throughout the universe – the kingdom of God.

Our true self was originally created in Heaven's consciousness. Born with a free will, we choose to become one through God's Love integrating our souls.

I am an active part of your evolution of spirit, and you are with me as we change the course of nature; we know that we are one in spirit, and we are evolving together. Being transformed one day at a time, we become aware of our progress in Heaven's firmament. Our white flame of hope builds our essence and reminds us of our liberation. Our soul is as a butterfly flowing in the wind of the Holy Spirit's Love.

There are two kinds of scientists doing research: Fixed, mainstream Westerners stand on financial statistics; and then there are the enlightened ones. All who are receptive of the idea of eternal life after physical death find insight and wisdom from their higher authority. Together, faithful souls are the collective consciousness that is lifting awareness of the whole earth.

As our spiritual Love arises, we merge. The light of pure consciousness aligns with great minds into the collective consciousness.

Socrates, Plato, Aristotle, Einstein, Max Planck, and Rupert Sheldrake were all persuaded that our lives are divinely guided and influenced. Those who have had near-death experiences support this common sense as well.

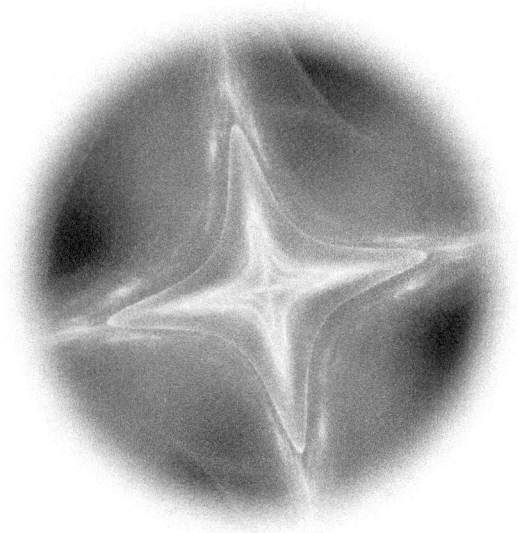

Timing

While the signs of the times speak disaster
Heaven sends angels, God's divine harvester
To take departing souls away from the sinister
Our hearts in harmony know a sweet mystery
God's spiritual resilience lives in you and me
The breath of light is our spiritual liberty
Our Holy Spirit guides our soul
Our spirits ascend as our Love unfolds
In the light of Heaven's Love we behold
Our family in Paradise, our joy untold
Perfectly sacred, eternally whole

23

Science Has Come Full Circle

Long ago, scientists believed that intelligence was the light within humanity's consciousness that influenced the universe. Our scientific forefathers came to the same conclusions of today's recent scientists. Quantum theory researchers use high-powered microscopes to learn the behavior of our cells, to report that living behavior is much the same as our universe.

"Old science" believed what Einstein said:

> Scientific research is based on the assumption that all events, including the actions of mankind, are determined by the laws of nature [creation]. Therefore, a research scientist will hardly be inclined to believe that events could be influenced by a prayer, that is, by a wish addressed to a supernatural being. However, we have to admit that our actual knowledge of these laws is only an incomplete piece of work [unvollkommenes Stückwerk], so that ultimately the belief in the existence of fundamental, all-embracing laws also rests on a sort of faith. All the same, this faith has been largely justified by the success of science. On the other hand, however, every-

one who is seriously engaged in the pursuit of science becomes convinced that the laws of nature manifest the existence of a spirit vastly superior to that of men, and one in the face of which we with our modest powers must feel humble....The pursuit of science leads therefore to a religious feeling of a special kind, which differs essentially from the religiosity of more naive people.

*With friendly greetings,
your Albert Einstein*[1]

Einstein expresses how the laws in creation and the belief in the existence of the fundamental, all-embracing laws rest on faith in the spirit, which is vastly superior to our own. The pursuit of science leads to a special kind of spiritual awareness that is not found in religiosity. God's breath of life is the vastly superior spirit that has birthed gracious families into creation.

For over two thousand years, exquisite celestial armies, or in biblical terms, the kingdom of Heaven, is ever present to support and nurture our spiritual evolution.

We are called to bask in the winds of our Holy Spirit in the womb of Love as we are transcending this earthly body one breath at a time. Our soul is becoming a prism of our pure consciousness in the Creator's intelligent design. Our magnanimously brilliant character is being formed in the image of God as together we are cocreating and forming our own personalities.

Scientists may understand what causes the formation of a snowflake or a crystal or the growth of an organism, but science has yet to explain how the pattern of a snowflake is symmetrically or geometrically perfect and appears precise in structure and continuity. To make a symmetrically blooming crystal, the purity of nature's diamond, a geometrically perfect snowflake, a tiny rosebud, or the morphallaxis character of a monarch butterfly, one must be a creator.

"*The unfolding of your words gives light; it is understanding to the simple*" (Psalms 119:130). I am happy to know my higher authority is forming our consciousnesses. In continuity, our spiritual connection is articulating our countenances and our circumstances to bring pure justice, which is divine order. "The fruit of righteousness is the tree of life" (Proverbs 11:30). We are intricately involved in an elaborate composition of celestial beings in the Heavens.

Many good scientists have gathered the courage to make an effort to answer many questions. More curiosity arises as a result of the thousands of near-death reports. When the brain has flatlined and the heart is not functioning, how can consciousness remain cognitive? The answer is that while we are present here on earth, we're also alive in our Creator's spiritual consciousness.

When our spirit rises from this mortal body, we are raptured from this material world. Our extended spiritual family peacefully guides us home. When death of the physical body expels it, the soul journeys into a spiritual dimension. Each near-death experience is a different expression of each individual unique soul.

People who experience near-death share their reflections of the light source being that of their native origin. The source of Love that people first experience imprints the way that their soul identifies Heaven's Love. Whether through a loved one or through a spiritually transformative experience in the light of a celestial being, the impact leaves an imprint of that particular source and becomes their *being of light*.

It has been documented that a certain percent of people who have NDEs are distressed and go into a dark or detached place, an abyss where hell is for real. "Everlasting" means "timeless" in translation from the Greek. The Hebrew word for "lightning" was "fire"; hell's torment is described as a place of loneliness and anguish in a timeless fire. Many who had near-death experiences witnessed hell and came back because a White Light of true Love reached out for their acceptance.

A configuration of light enables the lost to return and share their revitalization or salvation; their message is, "I saw a White Light." Many distressed, near-death experiencers of hell's consciousness say that they see a White Light that conveys pure acceptance and Love.

From that time forward, while here on earth what was a distressed soul becomes spiritually aware of the peaceful presence bringing a message of Love.

Heaven's Consciousness

To most, God with us is the light in Jesus Christ. Many people report receiving the light of life and healing all at one time from him. Worldwide reports show that spiritual consciousness becomes aware in another dimension. Spiritual consciousness includes understanding new feelings beyond the physical limitations we describe as love or a beloved friend.

The most common, residual message near-death experiences return with is, "It is not your time."

Everyone who returns with the message, "It is not your time," also returns with a personal realization of being eternally valued in the light of the pure consciousness of divine Love.

This message does say, "It is your time or your turn to develop pure consciousness." We are given this time as a gift of life. We are given a free will to utilize our willpower and create the essence of our eternal soul. We are interconnected and grow in our Garden of Life.

This life is our turn in time to develop moral and spiritual stability. Our life is here to fulfill our Love covenant on earth as it is in Heaven. Together in Heaven's consciousness, our whole family tree evolves.

There are well over two thousand documented near-death-experience case reports that undeniably prove the authenticity of consciousness after passing. It is not thought possible to explain near-death reports only in terms of physiological processes. The conclusion to this occurrence is that all of one's consciousness is not only located in the brain.

Because of the controversy surrounding spiritually transforming experiences, physicians and scientists have written many books. NDEs raise questions that some modern, mainstream scientists are beginning to answer.

The facts are there, but it is curious to me how some people desire to gather details of actual NDE reports only to discredit them. What is most disturbing to me is that particular scientists go to great efforts to disregard the real statistics. Rather than discovering their own consciousnesses are living in a divine spiritual law in this living universe—on earth as it is in Heaven—their efforts seem to lean more toward qualifying for certain educational grants or being supported by the pharmaceutical dynasties.

Long before bad science had a chokehold on academics, and long before the truth was made into religions, people nurtured one another. Communities helped one another as they watched the intricacies of their summer gardens grow enough food to share for a year. They knew there was a valuable spiritual mystery in their lives that was supported in creation. They shared their harvest along with spiritual love for equality and the goodness of how things work out for the best. In loyalty and respectful friendships, they knew that keeping good morality and ethics helped all relationships.

In caring for one another, they received spiritual guidance. Their joys in life came in loving one another with the Love they received from above. Their ancestral, celestial Tree of Life was rooted in their spiritual values and moral equality.

Through creation and through the spirit of Love, God redefines perfection to reveal to each one of us individually our path to enlightenment. God's devotion in creation is intricately woven within our heart's deep Loving intentions. Our own Holy Spirit's sacred relationships is our unifying process with Heaven's consciousness. This and the power of prayer cannot be proven by science. Love awareness, along with emotional and spiritual attachments, have yet to be validated by skeptical scientists.

The essence of life in the way that a butterfly transforms from a caterpillar is a mystery in the laws of creation. We, too are intertwined in the universe's womb, here to live to Love. "He keeps his mind in perfect peace whose mind is stayed on you because he trusts in you" (Isaiah 26:3).

Great minds think alike regardless of their times. We have come full circle in the truisms that were accepted before doctrinal guidelines existed.

Note

1. Einstein Archives at the National and University Library in Jerusalem and the Library of the Union Theological Seminary in New York. "To Phyllis Wright," January 24, 1936. In Calaprice's, Dear Professor Einstein, pp. 128–29. Einstein Archives, pp. 42–602.

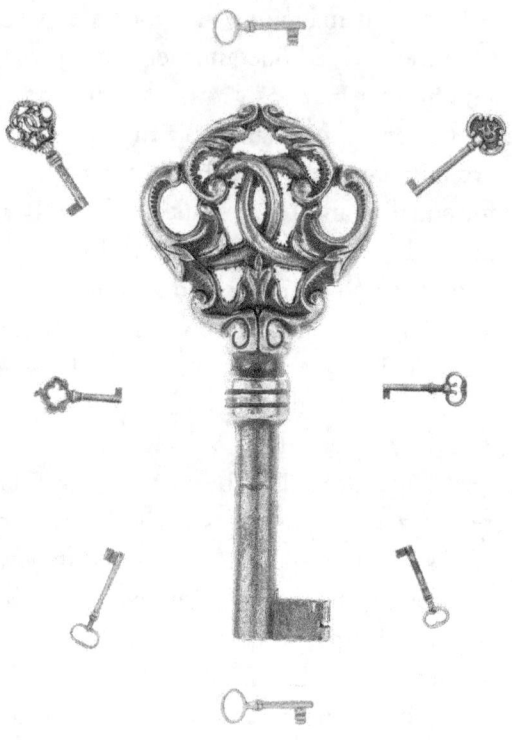

My Key

Courage is found on solid ground
In the brilliance of God's integrity
Love never dies; truth lights up lives
Spirit leads the heart into stability
In justice we find mercy
The Holy Spirit abounds faithfully
Through intuition and in sensitivity
Divine wisdom becomes a reality
We trust and stand quietly
To listen very carefully
Discovering truth intrinsically
Until ignited courageously
The Holy Spirit is our omnipotent key
We're one in the light of God's deity

24

Prayer: A Challenge for Science

- Since ancient times, a strong and pervasive belief in the efficacy of prayer–for the living and the dead–reinforces the notion that consciousness is not limited to the physical body. Not only do traditions throughout the world share a belief that prayers may in some way help (or invoke help from) deceased ancestors, many cultures throughout history have believed that prayer can bring about changes in the physical circumstances of the living. If prayer affects things in the physical world, its effects should be measurable, and science should be able to investigate it. There is a very scattered literature on this, but when you bring it all together as Larry Dossey has done in his recent book, Healing Words (Harper San Francisco, 1993), you see there is quite a large number of interesting experiments with challenging results. Out of 131 controlled experiments on prayer-based healing, more than half showed statistically significant benefits. One of the best known is a double-blind study of 393 patients in the coronary unit at San Francisco General Hospital. In this experiment,

192 patients, chosen at random, were prayed for by home-prayer groups, the others were not. The prayed-for patients recovered better than the controls, and fewer died. In order to make sense of these data on the efficacy of prayer, science will have to change its underlying assumptions about the nature of causality. Currently, the standard view is still purely mechanistic–notwithstanding all the recent talk about chaos and complexity theory. When applied to the life sciences, chaos and complexity theory–even with the help of highly sophisticated computer modeling–still explain the world in terms of mechanical causes involving known physical and chemical processes. The data from empirical studies of prayer, as well as from the large literature reporting psi research in telepathy, clairvoyance, and psychokinesis, seriously challenge the mechanistic view. Some other causal agent besides the mechanics of electrochemical interactions is required to make sense of the observed phenomena. Holistic thinkers generally divide into two main categories. The majority want to have holism on the cheap. They want a holism which doesn't conflict with science as we know it. Instead of exploring the possibility of new causal factors, they prefer to explain holism in terms of complexity and self-organization of conventional mechanical forces, modeled with sophisticated mathematics and the latest computer techniques. Nothing essentially different from physical and chemical interactions is considered to account for the properties of living systems. The other group of holists, a minority among which I include myself and Larry Dossey, think that there is more to it than just what we know about chemistry and physics and clever mathematical models. My view is that there are other causal factors in nature, processes that make actual differences–causes in nature which bring about new kinds of effects that we have to take into account in order to understand our experience and the world. These new causal factors are involved in things like paranormal phenomena, prayer, and healing. The whole thrust of my morphic resonance theory is to say there is more to nature than just the standard forces in physics. And what's more, *these other agents are at the very heart of the way things are organized in chemistry, in life, and in consciousness.*

- **Prayer and Mental Fields** *How might prayer fit in with the scientific view of things? I shall focus on two broad categories of prayer: petitionary and intercessory. In petitionary prayer, we ask for something for ourselves; in intercessory prayer, we pray to a higher power for the benefit of other people (either living or dead). In praying for other people and for ourselves, we ask a higher power to bring about a particular result. For me, this is what distinguishes prayer from positive thinking. Positive thinking involves nothing more than one's own mind, one's own desires and wishes, but petitionary and intercessory prayer are put in the context of a higher power. For this reason, positive thinking does not fit into the category of prayer—even though it is often confused with it. Whether petitionary or intercessory, prayer clearly poses a challenge to the mechanistic view of the world. According to this view, there is no way that thoughts going on in your head, which at most create small electrochemical disturbances barely detectable a few inches from your head even by highly sensitive apparatus, could affect someone or something at a remote distance. If you were practicing positive thinking or some of the more specifically directed forms of petitionary prayer, you could resort to explanations in terms of telepathy, or if it were a prayer affecting physical objects, you might say it was psychokinesis. But such explanations serve only to replace one set of explanations which lie outside the scope of modern mechanistic science with another set. There is nothing in mechanistic science that could allow mere thoughts inside my mind, whether cast in the form of prayer or as positive thinking, to affect things at a distance. It just can't happen. The key to understanding prayer as a scientific phenomenon requires, in my view, getting away from the idea of the mind as somehow inside the brain. If we think our minds are confined to our brains—the standard view—then since what goes on in our brain occurs in the privacy and isolation of our own skull, it can't affect anyone* *else. However, I see minds being fieldlike in nature (part of my general view of morphic fields), and I see mental fields as the basis for habitual patterns of thought. Mental fields go beyond, through, and interface with the electromagnetic patterns in the brain. In this way, mental fields can affect our bodies through our brains. However, they are much more extensive than our brains, reaching out to great distances in some cases. As soon as we have the idea that the mind can be extended through these mental fields, and over large distances, we have a medium of connection through which the power of prayer could work. We are no longer dealing with a purely mechanical system in the brain, with absolutely no way of connecting the brain and the observed effect—for if that were the case, the phenomenon of effective prayer would have to be dismissed as delusion or coincidence. With a mental field, however, we have a medium for a whole series of connections between us and the people, animals, and places we know and care about—with the rest of the world, in fact. When we pray, those extended mental fields would be the context in which prayer could work nonlocally.*

- **Nonlocalized Mind** *Clearly, this does not amount to a fully articulated scientific theory of prayer; it is highly speculative. But, I believe, it is also very clear that we need to have a much broader view of how the mind is extended beyond the brain. We need a theory of what I call the "extended mind" as opposed to the conventional scientific view of the "contracted mind" holed up inside the skull. This view of a contracted mind came from Descartes in the seventeenth century. It is a model of consciousness which separates our minds from the whole world around us into a small region in the brain—a model of the mind which plainly contradicts direct experience. For example, when you see this page in front of you, you experience it as being outside you, not inside your brain. To say that this and all your other perceptions are located in your brain is a theory, not an experience. It is important, however, not to envisage the extended mind as some amorphous field, a kind of undifferentiated Universal Mind.*

I don't think we should make a large leap from the concept of a contracted mind to a boundless universal mind. Such a jump isn't helpful scientifically. My idea of morphic fields is that even though they are extended and nonlocal in their effects, they are still part of our individual and collective mind, but not to be equated with some ultimate Universal Mind. The morphic fields are not God. They are nonlocal in the sense that they can spread out over immense distances (as, for instance, gravitational fields do), so that if I were praying about somebody in Australia from my home in London the morphic field would carry the information and the prayer could work. But my mental field wouldn't usually spread out to Mars, for example, because there is nothing connecting me to someone on that planet. If someone I knew had traveled there on a spaceship, then there would be a link. For morphic fields to have a mental connection, I believe there has to be something that links you to the other person. Even if you have never met the other person, I believe just knowing their name or something about them seems to be enough to establish a connection, though this connection is likely to be weaker than that between people who know each other well. You could picture it something like this: When two people come into contact and establish some mental connection (perhaps experienced as affection, love, even hate) their morphic fields in effect become part of a larger, inclusive field. Then, if they separate from each other, it is as if their particular portions of the morphic field are stretched elastically, so that there remains a "mental tension" or link between them. There has to be something like this that relates the two people.

- **Nested Sets of Morphic Fields** *Morphic fields are organized in nested hierarchies. For example, there are morphic fields surrounding the atoms in our bodies, which are within the higher-level morphic fields of molecules, organelles, cells, organs, and limbs, all of which exist within the morphic field associated with the entire body. The body field, in turn, would be within the field of relationships that constitute a family within a larger social group. Societies, in* *turn, are embedded within ecosystems, and ecosystems within in the planetary system, "Gaia." And by extrapolation, we could extend the series of nested morphic fields until we reach out beyond planetary, solar system, and galactic limits to encompass the entire universe. Even Einstein's space-time field of gravitation is a universal, cosmic field holding everything together and linking the entire universe, in fact, making it a universe. It does the same thing as the World Soul or Anima Mundi of neo-Platonic philosophy. It embraces the whole cosmos. There are levels upon levels of morphic fields within fields, within which we are embedded. Human life is embedded in vastly larger fields of organization. To what degree they are conscious still remains in the realm of speculation. But I would assume that higher-level fields are not less, and probably more, conscious than we are. I would think they are more conscious than we are not simply because they are larger in size, but because they are more inclusive, contain more complexity, and encompass more possibilities. I think that is one way of interpreting traditional doctrines about superhuman intelligences, or cosmic intelligences, usually thought of in Christianity as the hierarchy of the angels. The word "angel" normally conveys the image of a good-looking youth with wings; but that's simply a pictorial representation. The traditional doctrine behind that image, however, is of a superhuman intelligence. And if the solar system and galaxy have intelligence, then one might be an angel and the other an archangel. In some traditional Christian doctrines there are, for instance, nine hierarchies of angels or levels of intelligence. And I would see these as equivalent to intelligences, minds or organizing fields at different levels of complexity. The galactic angels, for instance, would embrace or include those of solar systems, which in turn would include those of planets. This is a description of a cosmos which has intelligence at every level, not a view that sees consciousness as something that emerged from unconscious matter. Conscious intelligence was there to start with. The place to look for it is not going to be in atoms or quanta (although there*

> *may be some kind of consciousness there), but in solar systems and galaxies and in the whole cosmos. There may be all these different levels of imagination, intelligence, and mind throughout the whole of the cosmic organization. All traditional doctrines that I know of have recognized something of that kind.*[1]

Rupert's article offers us a scientific explanation on the energy fields of prayer. In my view, he suggests that archangels and saints are the hierarchies that stabilize our planetary systems. I understand this to mean that our universe holds collective consciousness, which are nested sets of spiritual, morphic fields. I also think these morphic fields can include the practicing and creation of paranormal phenomena. These fields can include some less-intelligent levels of spiritual consciousness as well as more refined dimensions of Heaven's consciousness.

Then, there is the question of not having or having faith. How can one believe that prayer works without faith, through psychokinesis? Here we see that spiritual sensitivity or having an ability to move in the spirit can be accomplished through mental powers alone. To believe that through willpower alone things can be moved without knowing the Creator is to not understand the laws of creation.

The collective consciousness of the faithful, from my experience, is understood through various expressions of our Creator's Love. The Holy Spirit can be explained as the morphic resonance or the light of Heaven's consciousness.

By free choice, one can be willing to open one's heart and soul to believe or become interconnected with his or her Creator and the source of understanding faith.

Let's explore the idea of faith or belief in a God of Love and how this influences spiritual awareness. Without Love, one can only have a vague understanding of a mysterious God.

Love for others is a form of intercessory prayer and is interconnecting with the morphic fields of others and by faith, bringing them into the light of one's own spiritual aptitude. When through our Holy Spirit we have Loving prayers for others, we are in intercessory prayer. Our words of faith are mainstreamed into the heart of creation, transforming our soul, evolving our spiritual life.

Heaven's complex, intelligent organization of our galactic solar system moves by our faithful relationships. Being creatures of habit and in tune with one another's morphic fields, we receive precognitions. We pray to preserve and uphold the faithful intensions of our collective consciousness or communities.

Fulfilling God's vision, given a free will, we depend on our support system of saints and angels. Our Holy Spirit is subliminally beaming intelligently, resonating with our Heavenly families. Our hierarchy is evolving us into the image of God. We experience new freedoms—spiritual emotions of true Love.

When a well-known and published scientist, in this case, Rupert Sheldrake, brings together two disciplines—conventional science with spiritual consciousness—there are defiant responses that come from mainstream media.

Paid skeptics want to keep a debate going much like the scribes and Pharisees. Also, people who accept the quick fix—religious dogmas—oppose or disregard the data that indicate the human soul is interconnected with its own higher consciousness. Illogical consciousness always resides in the furnace of a moral meltdown.

Clingers to false doctrines befall the worldly arrogance. When the truth resonates from a person's dignity, it frightens people who subscribe to man-made limits. Misery does love company as good scientific evidence is aborted in cynicism's irreverence; together, bad science is a propellant for confusion's smokescreen.

As the world turns from the global myriad of belief systems, light arises in our living universe. Our confidence and security in truisms, our values growing together, are the rational moral fiber of good common sense and are in sync with spiritual evolution.

While a war for collective consciousness rages, prayers coagulate in Heaven and become brighter. In peaceful comprehension, we are moved by compassion in the collective consciousness of our Lord's close friends. We share our intuitive premonitions telepathically responding to one another. God's spirit is our living message system, ushering in a new horizon for the dawning of a new day.

I believe that God sends consciousnesses from distant star systems to create intelligent humans. I believe that clarity of mind and spirit comes through the soul of celestial sons—angels and their children. These offspring of Heaven's consciousness glow in living color and retain their spiritual beauty while creating variations of divine order. Understanding this allows one to be interdimensional in thought and deed. By living this way, the path to Heaven is filled with discernible feelings and new discoveries.

I look at the mystery in the holographic consciousness of God, and it is the same mystery I find in my eternal soul and is the logical source of my creativity, one that I am unable to express outside of spirituality. We participate together in an innate Love, building a relationship, one with the Creator.

This is where our capability for amazement arises. Without our connection to Heaven's collective consciousness, we are in a state of doubt, as good as lifeless. Our innate memory is our inherent, morphic fields entangled with all of nature and every living creature on earth. We receive encouragement from Heaven's consciousness for our will to " power up." This feeling of spiritual sensibility gives us a sense of being alive and attentive; our aptitudes increase our adaptability as we rise from human energy fields into pure consciousness.

In all nationalities, true words bring light, transcending time into comprehensive consciousness, carrying understanding for all to receive their own way. In the beginning, God breathed the White Light, forming cognitive consciousness. Through the ages, this same river of eternal life carries the voices of the ancients through Scripture. This strengthens our spiritual consciousness; our moral backbone stabilizes our faith, and we can stand in peace.

Our spiritual character is becoming one with the divine will of our intelligent God. The light of spirit teaches us respect for our individual soul's holy extension in Heaven. Our spirit moves within God's spiritual laws as in the mind of Christ. Our integrity is developed within our soul through our choices; we are building our home in Heavenly places. God is revealing ways for us to accept, in divine timing, our own radiant Loveliness.

In spiritual evolution, we evolve from habitual, human love energy fields into courageous, spiritual lives. We were created to eventually accept and develop our own wills to evolve our personalities into our intended grand designs. By our souls' alignment with God, the central character of the universe is the organization of the cosmos, or as Max Planck says, "the matrix of all matter."

> *All matter originates and exists only by virtue of a force which brings the particle of an atom to vibration and holds this most minute solar system of the atom together. We must assume behind this force the existence of a conscious and intelligent mind. This mind is the matrix of all matter.*[2]

Max Planck, founder of quantum theory, is known for discovering the radiation law. Quantum physics explains how sunlight causes alignment in the energy fields of nature in much the same way conscious intentions or prayers change the course of nature and also affect energy fields. Today's enlightened scientists, aligned with God's "will," are bringing light through their intentions, transforming energy fields, and expanding spiritual truths. Through our souls, we are beaming our lights of "truth" from our conscious behaviors that emanate through our prisms when we are interconnected with the divine order of Heaven's consciousness.

Notes

1. Rupert Sheldrake PhD. (Summer, 1994). Prayer: A challenge for science. *Noetic Sciences Review, 30*, 4-9. http://www.sheldrake.org/Articles&Papers/papers/morphic/prayer.html
2. Max Planck, *Eight Lectures on Theoretical Physics* (Dover Publications, 1997). Max Planck (1858–1947) is a German theoretical physicist who originated quantum theory. In 1918, Planck received the Nobel Prize in Physics for his work in quantum theory. For an extended discussion of these theories, see the following by Rupert Sheldrake: *Science Set Free: 10 Paths to New Discovery; The Presence of the Past: Morphic Resonance and the Memory of Nature;* and *Morphic Resonance: The Nature of Formative Causation.* www.sheldrake.org/Resources/faq/answers.html; www.sheldrake.org

Intelligence

Our unity already formed before the day of Adam's seed
One God in the spirit speaks to every tongue and creed
On this ball of clay, we evolve into one Love and concede
One life to receive the essential Love we need
Our lives are one in spirit together we move indeed
We are gifted with this grace, in unity we succeed
One message system, a living universe in Godspeed
Heaven turns the time around for our soul to proceed

25

Trusting My New Paradigm

Where my physical heart carries the rhythm of my attitude, my spirit reflects the condition of my soul. Having experienced deeper dimensions opened my spiritual awareness and intensified my belief system. I returned from my adventure knowing we are all an extension of one another, spiritually bonded together. We understand that while we are living on earth our bodies are time based vessels for our souls to shape our destinies.

Since my twins were born, I have a deep understanding and knew for sure that they would be healthy and happy, just as I witnessed in Heaven. My vision of them came true precisely as I saw them when I traveled forward in time. I remember the day, the dress on my little girl, her golden red curls, and her little sandals. There she was, sitting patiently with a smile on her face, holding one toe, waiting for me to pick her up. Full of life and always optimistic, beaming with a bouncing smile, my son's heart bubbled over, full of giggles as he looked at me. Just as I saw them when I was in Heaven, there they sat, pleasantly waiting on me while enjoying one another.

My twins brought to mind and made me remember the presence of my Heavenly family. My beloved, intelligent twins could not fathom the Love that they generated in me while I was in Heaven. It dawned on me that while our glorious family awaits us, we, too are unable to fathom the Love we generate in Heaven.

At a very young age, I found my daughter Stephanie's accurate discernments mind boggling. Along with being the prettiest little girl around, she carried herself with confidence as she could see into a person's motives. My baby girl's insightful ways were pleasingly amiable and relaxed in a good environment but also served as an excellent alarm, a warning to us that we were in the wrong place. My son continued to keep us humble and observant with his sense of humor. Jonathan's happiness was contagiously wonderful. In the evenings, he would remind us to gather around and share our good experiences of the day. Of course, my young twins were intellectually unable to express the depth of their hearts, but I learned how to listen well to God's wisdom - "out of the mouth of babes" (Psalms 8:2).

Early on, the twins showed me the importance of listening past what people were saying by listening to their souls; little children are like that. I had the privilege of showing my twins how to confront serious issues, see past obstacles, and look on the bright side. What appears to be the foolishness of humanity may very well be God's sense of humor emphasizing the importance of gaining our trust.

As we align in divine Love, we are enlightened by our Holy Spirit and we are evolving together. I believed that God's tremendous sense of humor revealed the past tense of each negative encounter. Quickly, I would be reminded of how God specializes in the impossible to engage our full attention. Learning to listen well to my intuition built a spiritual awareness within me of the greater purpose in my life. While God holds our attention, we can laugh at our young egos in the awareness that tomorrow brings a new day to reflect on our innocent blunders of today. My eternal purpose outshines being a poet, an artist, and even a mom.

While in Heaven, I reviewed my life before I was born. Heaven is my origin, home, and my future. I didn't see nationalities, cultures, or locations but rather the colorful tempering process like that of sparkling jewels and precious metals. I was more centered on the outcome rather than the temporary process of life on earth.

Trusting My New Paradigm

My life review began with prebirth when I was one of our Creator's seeds, like an atom or a tiny larva of a butterfly. Within true Love's council, I discovered my free will; my gift of life. My life evolved in Heaven along with the lives of my neighbors and friends. Heaven's consciousness always involves the whole council of God's heart and reasons in the terms of Love's evolution.

In accordance with destiny, my time came. I, too, accepted my turn to enter a lifetime on earth. I selected a life to be challenged so that while I developed my will, I strengthened my Heavenly neighborhood to spiritually expand with creation. I am meant to fulfill my original purpose within God's grand design. This is my time to expand in the womb of the universe.

God prepared my soul to accept the truth even when it didn't feel good to my humanity. Time is on my side to excel in spiritual courage so that I can increase in the wisdom of my Holy Spirit.

By not being treated or recognized as equal, I can develop a strong conscience. My life of rude awakenings began as a young child not fitting in. On my way to Heaven, I was startled by the words of the imp, "You don't belong here!" As I reflected on this intimidating voice, I was reminded of many similar, confrontational events I weathered while on earth.

The spirit world is an organized battleground for energy fields. We all are placed in our own Garden of Eden and given a free will. On my elementary school playground, I felt this same intimidation coming through startling words. Another child, Joel, looked at me with his dark brown eyes and said, "We don't want to play with you!" This forever changed my paradigm. I began to realize that there was a lot more going on then what I could see on the surface.

On my way to elementary school, I wasn't allowed to walk on my side of the street. This same hateful voice came out of a mentally challenged child, "Get outta here or I will run over you!" Seemingly harmless words coming from a mentally challenged boy, but they were from a more sinister place, a source that pierced my soul and were meant to undermine my ability to love my neighbor as myself.

I was the only white girl who qualified to play on my high school basketball team where I was threatened by these same words, "Get away from us, we don't like you!" Two really big, tall girls told me to quit, so I did. I found assurance and courage in the fact that I would not be able to compete with them, anyway.

In the early years of my professional career, I was the only female salesperson. I outperformed the salesmen in four offices. Again, I was challenged with these same words. I saw that their failure was a result of their insatiable need to be successful. I discovered a new level of success in my dedication to serve rather than sell. In my quest to live a life in truth, I always found another open door.

I could go on and on, but my point is this: I did not quit nor was I a quitter just because I learned not to retaliate or to be confrontational but rather to take my leave from a place where there was hatred. Hindsight is twenty-twenty and reveals God's humor.

Heaven's intelligent, spiritual light is the breath of God. God builds within us an assurance that cannot be shaken. We find ourselves in what we consider difficult situations only to discover that God was there first.

I was first created in Heaven to cocreate my individuality by my willingness to be empowered by my Holy Spirit. Made in God's image, in faith, I am willing to live my life being a governess over my own willpower. I am aware of my Lord's presence and various energy fields in my environment. My willpower aligns with God's investment of faith within me. In my own rendering of divine Love, I will ascend in pure consciousness.

My Holy Spirit is my gift of eternal life and my measure of faith (Romans 12:3). My free will, created in the image of God, will grow in grace (II Peter 3:18). My conscience or morality, my ethical behavior, opens my heart to God's creative nature.

One cannot sin without first accepting pure consciousness or faith. "Sin" is to break or trespass the soul's established moral compass and to disregard life's purpose by turning away from the knowledge of right, to do wrong.

I make time to center within. In becoming one with my Holy Spirit, my thoughts are arranged in a fresh, new order. In my mind's eye, I see my consciousness growing with my celestial family tree, extending in Heaven's light to the far reaches of our universe.

I am humbled by God's Love when I am anchored in the multidimensional kingdom of Heaven. I trust in the absolute pure justice and protection of the Lord of Creation. In Heaven's Love is the divine order of saints; archangels are sent to us from our celestial families to encourage us to live in the present.

I am honored to receive understanding that God's divine order is expressed through creation in an indescribable intimate Love. As I accept the majestic ways of our Lord, *the cares of life* can cause me to open my heart in faith and pray in intercession.

Our firmament or Heaven is in the process of evolving our souls, expanding our homes in Paradise. *"He is like a tree planted by water, that sends out its roots by the stream, and it does not fear when heat comes, and its leaves remain green, and it is not anxious in the year of drought, for it does not cease to bear fruit"* (Jeremiah 17:08).

We, together are aligning our loved ones in a fresh, new healing peace. We are receiving help from above, moving forward with a band of angels on every side.

In the light of God's Love, we do not allow misery to visit with us, behaving as if we are the savior of the world, but rather we dwell in the light of timeless truths that burn away evil. Dark clouds dissipate as my spiritual awareness rises up in knowledge and archangels intervene. What appears as difficulties may truly be opportunities for faith to expand with the infinite. I become one in the truth, the life, and the way that I, too can say to our Lord, *"Rest right here until I make your enemies, your foot-stool"* (Psalms 110:1, Matthew 22:44).

By free will, I accept God's gift of grace in my soul's connection with you. In spirit, we are interwoven and expanding with our residences in Heaven. We trust the Creator to draw us together into harmony with pure consciousness as one with our Heavenly family.

My darling daughter and gentle son were honor roll students all through junior high and high school and earned degrees from Trinity University. Both have furthered their educations and brought their enthusiasm and Love for life into our Garden of Life. Both are youth leaders. Both are happily married with healthy children. And I am a happy, adoring grandmother.

Precious Souls

One rainbow hoops the sky for miles
A splendid sight to see
Light is shining from the stars
Engages our curiosity
God sees our true reaction
Our heart felt appreciation
For the laws of spirit within creation
As the sky reflects a grandeur majesty
Of an omniscient Lord sharing a mystery
How marvelous is this colorful array
Someday will carry us to eternity
In our elegant wonder, these gifts are free
Does our reaction build our destiny?
God gives comfort to humanity
We know our childlike faith
Amends poor reason, and still we see
While being held to reality
By good judgment and gravity
We are an extension of infinity
As Love gently nurtures us to grow
From wonderment comes a peace we know
In God's grace, we love life's quest
We share deep joy, laughing and sighing
Loving and learning to find our best
Until we are out of breath

26

Our Conclusion Is Heaven's Consciousness

As good science has revealed through the study of near-death experiences, our consciousness extends outside of the physical body. A temporary receiver we call the brain provides our navigation skills as our ego sorts to form choices that become our personal attitudes. Our spiritual consciousness is, most of the time, receptive to Heaven's messengers without our intellectual prompting, just as our human body heals itself without our awareness.

We enjoy our unique ego being blessed with insight, giving us freedom in the process of creating our own personalities. My real peace in living is the assurance that we are in the right place in the right time, reflecting our true essence.

We see the collective consciousness of human energy fields nested in habitual restlessness, devouring lives through indulgences. This is because people are avoiding their spiritual premonitions—disregarding the fact that they are causing their own cravings.

Sometimes, we must withdraw in order to spend quality time alone. Angels open our spiritual ears and eyes as we respond; we are cocreating our higher positioning in the cosmos. As we receive the Love of God, we accept being a fruitful, enlightened soul—a resonating star of many colors on the Tree of Life, building and expanding our Lord's domain in our universe.

With an increased Love for the Creator, we are helping one another to our home. Earth's spiritual journey accelerates our conscious evolution even though most of the time we are unaware of our progress. Life reveals more excellence each step of the way, enabling us to reason with the infinite.

In Heaven, we experience a more comprehensive intelligence and find ourselves dancing in the graces with our celestial family. Our expressions of grace glow as stars shining in an array of colorful symmetrical light prisms in the pulse of God's Love.

My Heavenly family and I have traveled together from our beginning. Everyone in Paradise is transparently aware that we are progressing together in God's intelligent music. Gradually merging together, one turn at a time, we evolve one another in the ascension of life. In Heaven, we have hyperclarity. I spent about forty minutes in Heaven with friends and relatives, and we were all familiar with our origins.

Every living soul that originated in Heaven will search until it locates and unites, becoming one with the Holy Spirit, the gift of life— our personal Comforter who is guiding us to move as one in spirit.

The expansion of our soul is instrumental in this cocreation within the divine timing of our Lord. Aligning our priorities in the venue of true Love, we gain spiritual fortitude. The Holy Spirit gives us insight, devising our way to maturity in wisdom's perfection. We become one as we are merging together to evolve our own soul's unique Love expression.

The author of life gently engages our full attention by a presence of Loving acceptance, revealing our genuine value through Heaven's protection and guidance. In time alone in the secret place of the most high, we are bathed in the Love of God's river of life. We do not try to burst through an artery by repeatedly reminding God of our condition, but rather we keep our hearts in tune.

I am humbled in discovery of my eternal involvement with my Heavenly family. I am conscious of the Holy Spirit's omniscience in my living presence, fulfilling my understanding. Heaven's nurturing life increases my sensitivities and expands my awareness. My ego lives in a deep reverence and in a wonderful wonder of my higher spiritual connection; my consciousness becomes filled with vitality that comes from beyond earthly matters.

"My Lord, I thank you for my intuition that lights up my life today on earth as it is in Heaven. Every day, I am delighted with new understanding giving me insight and new courage. Thank you for teaching me how wonderful life is. For strength, we receive your wisdom from Heaven. Thank you for Immanuel, the light of the world, who reveals day by day how precious we are to our Loved ones, even in Heaven. I accept my Holy Spirit and turn away from this world's temporary distractions. Because of your Love for me, my trust grows deeper each day."

In sharing with you, I hope you, too are now aware that by being alive in the physical world, you're living in connection with the spiritual world. Perhaps you have discovered and are receptive to your own spiritual being and are in synch with the kingdom of Heaven. In your new hope to live every day of your life with this new perspective, you will discover inspiration and courage from Heaven to complete this life's everyday tasks.

In accepting your true, higher moral compass, you trust your spiritual intuition, your higher authority, and find you are in harmony with God's will. By living your life this way, you are building your eternal home.

Our Holy Spirit is in the current of living water flowing from the throne. Our Heavenly home emerges in a gorgeous fragrance, blooming life, as the water lily resting on the branches of the Tree of Life. We are rising together, loving our neighbor as ourselves. In our Creator's perfection, we are in a beautification process, shining as stars, sharing our light's fragrances and resonating our own uniqueness with one another.

Everyone who receives the light of his or her Holy Spirit shall ultimately find their original home in the celestial Tree of Life. Within our intimate relationship, God's wisdom provides peaceful ways, graces to nurture and fulfill us all the way, unfolding our life's original purpose, one day at a time. "Then the righteous (light of truth) will shine like the sun in the kingdom of their Father. He who has ears let him hear" (Matthew 13:43).

Living Song of Solomon's sings, "Who is this who looks down like the dawn, beautiful as the moon, bright as the sun, awesome as an army of (lights) banners?" (Song 6:10).

The light of living water rains into my soul, springing up new horizons in spiritual collective consciousness on earth as it is in Heaven. We shine as intelligent planets in concert with spiritual evolution. Resonating in the physical reality, our heart of hearts is in harmony with God. Armies of angels clear the way while revealing God's spirit is expanding through our consciousness.

Spiritual courage is revived by the spoken word just as the unfolding of a lily is an expression of Love to bless the Lord.

Our universe is made up of ego's (morphic) energy fields filled with resonating vibrations. When we find the truth about who we are in spirit, our souls can become as lights in Heaven's consciousness, resonating tones that create a symphony in harmony with Heaven. Love's divine orchestration of pure wisdom is pouring out on us—the living universe of endearing Love is the White Light helping us move into position in the Garden of Life, in the kingdom of Heaven.

God's spirit is simple unification not separate from our higher omnipotent Comforter that is continually bringing to our memory understanding of our intuition guided by our spiritual senses.

Our oneness in spiritual consciousness is dancing with creation in currents of light like a monarch butterfly flying in community toward perfect excellence. Gently whisking our attentiveness into God's consciousness, we answer by responding to our personal Loving intuition. Our wishes and prayers bring together our Heavenly families who are supportive of our spiritual life. Everyone who thirsts to harmonize with the will of the Father comes to the center of the heart of God.

Make sacred a time to reach from your inner light in anticipation of the expansion of your spiritual awareness. Discover how to listen well to Love. Find your value within yourself, which is precious, and accept that your higher Holy Spirit is eternal. This is undeniable.

Receive realization that your life is being intimately orchestrated in the tender Love of God. Know that you are joined with your original family in a higher spiritual realm.

As we receive a more compassionate Love, we learn to listen well in patience. Every mistake that we learn from is a stepping stone leading to our eternal wholeness. We are all learning to adapt to consciously keep in step to a higher tune with our trustworthy Lord.

Abiding in the presence of God, we are dwelling in adoration in the secret place of the most high and under protection of the Almighty (Psalms 91).

We trust explicitly in being one with our Lord who in Love reigns throughout eternity. In the dynasty of our Heavenly tree, our soul's growth is increasing our horizon, enlarging our glorious radiance. Our Love antennas move by our free will in harmony with our spiritual intuition in keeping our heart aware of truth as it is meant for us.

We are discovering divine Love in pure brilliance, peacefully evolving our souls. The most comfortable home accepted by God was the one that Solomon built, *"God gave Solomon wisdom beyond measure, and largeness of heart (conciousness), even as the sand that is on the sea shore"* (1 King 4:29).

Documented science is discovering that our universe is made up of energy fields and spiritual cognitive levels of intelligence that extend throughout the universe. In the spiritual realm, our energy fields are transformed by our will to Love. The light that gives life to our universe is filling it with the responses from our souls. Each individual's colorful, living, spiritual prism is engaged in the perfect orchestration of Heaven's consciousness. We are becoming brighter as we grow in grace with the precious jewels in the crown of glory shining in the vibrato of Heaven.

We align in the splendor of our soul's Heavenly extension and discover our consciousness is in a smoother transition as we receive pure wisdom. Woven in our living universe in Love's grand design are our life's chords—living, colorful melodies. Springing up are our own fountains, rivers of living water as Love is flowing from our hearts. Gifted with eternal life within the flow of Paradise's harmonic Loving melody, our attitudes create music, giving our Heavenly families new joy. They are dancing to our tune in divine timing.

Daily, we can move forward toward the fullness of our destiny to discover a new realm, a more vibrant, clean clarity, by fine-tuning our spiritual awareness. New Love floods our intuition in our revelation of the immensity of God. Brilliant Heavenly bodies, gracious jewels, shine into our hearts so we can become creative, glowing away the darkness by bringing new Love to life. "And they that are wise shall shine as the brightness of the firmament; and they shall turn many to righteousness (right thinking) as the stars forever and ever" (Daniel 12:3).

Much like the innate nature of a monarch butterfly—first a dome-shaped ornament, then through discipline, becoming a cocoon that ultimately transcends and pierces through its bondage to live on the fragrances of flowers—we, too finally and spiritually spread our wings. We, too are morphing into oneness with our eternal residence in our original domain. We fulfill our life's purpose each day as the cares of this life that were once thorns in Immanuel's crown are graced with our new courage. We are raptured in the light of Heaven's living jewels.

Humanity held by earthly matter is being affected by the cares of life only to be fully effective with the master builder of our divine, eternal soul. Life comes with a new zeal in our dawning of this new day. We're learning how to expand in true Love, and in this way we're fulfilling our life's purpose.

Our consciousness gives rise with our Heavenly hierarchies who take position in Heaven's gigantic choir, orchestrating creation. "When the morning stars sang together, and all the sons of God shouted for joy" (Job 38:7).

Our Lord and crown of glory, the bright and morning star, is shining brighter in a glowing grace. *"We have the prophetic word more fully confirmed, to which you will do well to pay attention as to a lamp shining in a dark place, until the day dawns and the morning star rises in your hearts"* (2 Peter 1:19). We grow in a deep, inner knowing of pure conscious peace.

We were originally designed to live and move and have our

being abundantly and above what we may ask or think. The more that we are mindful of our spiritual senses reasoning together, the more we experience the joy of becoming one in the purity of Heaven's consciousness. Amen.

Heaven's Consciousness

The Mind of the Spirit

Every morning brings a new horizon
From the shadows of my life
First to open my heart to Heaven
So my spirit comes alive
I close out all distraction
To remember my Lord's pure Love
Quiet in Heaven's consciousness
I receive help from above
In a sacred deep devotion
God's presence of light revives
Nurtured by pure wisdom
I recall the goodness in my life
Before my heart receives
My spirit alive believes
I trust the Lord of creation
To give me insight and direction
Then my family in the Heaven
Warms my heart with peace

THE END

Rhonda Nell is most acclaimed as an artist and a poet. Her work is a pure delight for everyone who loves natural beauty.

www.GracesHeaven.com

Glossary

Angel
Modern: Heavenly Spirit
Hebrew: Stout, Strong
Greek: Being
Inclusive of definitions: Interdimensional celestial

Arch Angel
Modern: Heavenly messenger
Hebrew: God
Greek: Chief
Inclusive of definitions: Hierarchy being

Celestial
Modern: Supremely good
Hebrew: Arch Angels: offspring
Greek: Heavenly Abode
Inclusive of definitions: Spiritual consciousness

Brilliant
Modern: Vivid, Glowing
Hebrew: God, Michael, Gabriel
Greek: Valiant warrior
Inclusive of definitions: Omni present Intelligence

Devil
Modern: Evil
Hebrew: Imp (cannibal)
Greek: False accuser; Deceiver, Imposter
Inclusive of definitions: Destroyer of life; Interdimensional spirit

Divine
Modern: Attributes
Hebrew: Observe experience
Greek: God consciousness
Inclusive of definitions: Order in symmetry

Eternity

Modern: Endless
Hebrew: Perpetually
Greek: Time does not rule
Inclusive of definitions: Living forever

Extra Terrestrial

Modern: Earth/sky being
Inclusive of definitions: Spirit; Earth and sky

Faith

Modern: Confidence in credibility
Hebrew: Established
Greek: Persuade
Inclusive of definitions: Acceptance of eternal life

Firmament

Modern: Expansion of Heaven
Hebrew: Extension of sky
Inclusive of definitions: Breathing light into creation

Feeling

Modern: Emotional impression
Hebrew: Search to know
Greek: Empathetic
Inclusive of definitions: Sensitive reaction

God

Modern: Eternal
Hebrew: Mighty Angel Father
Greek: Divine
Inclusive of definitions: Spirit in creation

Grace

Modern: Beauty of Creation
Greek: Gift
Inclusive of definitions: An ability to understand God

Heaven

Modern: Abode of Supreme

Hebrew: Sky; Air
Greek: Above
Inclusive of definitions: Multidimensional universe

Hierarchy

Modern: Order in authority
Inclusive of definitions: High intellectual authority

Holy

Modern: Made sacred, Separate
Hebrew: Dedicated to be hallowed
Greek: Divine character
Inclusive of definitions: To make or consider Godly

Immanuel

Modern: Emmanuel
Hebrew: Almighty God with us
Greek: Highest authority
Inclusive of definitions: White Light consciousness

Jesus

Modern: Divine Magistrate
Hebrew: From: Patriarch
Greek: Messiah
Inclusive of definitions: Comforter; Teacher

Christ

Modern: Manifestation of God
Hebrew: Not found Old Testament
Greek: Anointed Savior
Inclusive of definitions: Name given Immanuel

Kingdom

Modern: Territory
Hebrew: Empire
Greek: Royal Reign
Inclusive of definitions: Orchestration of authority

Knowledge

Modern: Information
Hebrew: Understanding

Greek: Sound reasoning
Inclusive of definitions: Intellectual development

Life

Modern: Experience
Hebrew: Heart
Greek: Revival
Inclusive of definitions: The beginning of the living

Light

Modern: Luminous
Hebrew: Happiness to ascend; Clarity
Greek: Kindle revelation
Inclusive of definitions: God consciousness

Love

Modern: Devotion
Hebrew: Gentle
Greek: Willingly embrace
Inclusive of definitions: God's expressions in Life

Omnipotent

Modern: Universal power
Hebrew: (Magistrate) Solid
Greek: Whiteness
Inclusive of definitions: All knowing presence

Omniscient

Modern: Infinite understanding
Inclusive of definitions: Creation is alive everywhere

Soul

Modern: Rational emotional faculty
Hebrew: To eat or be eaten
Greek: To breathe
Inclusive of definitions: Eternal consciousness of life

Spirit

Modern: Seat of emotions
Hebrew: Breath; Wind
Greek: Gather to assembly

Inclusive of definitions: Interconnection with Life

Truth

Modern: Belief it is true
Hebrew: Rational mind
Greek: Quality
Inclusive of definitions: Individual God awareness

Virtue

Modern: Goodness
Hebrew: Faith's ability
Greek: Love
Inclusive of definitions: Pure consciousness

Wisdom

Modern: Experience
Hebrew: Stout hearted
Greek: Higher/Lower; Intelligence
Inclusive of definitions: Implementing the knowledge of God

www.ingramcontent.com/pod-product-compliance
Lightning Source LLC
Chambersburg PA
CBHW050537300426
44113CB00012B/2153